AI&U

Translating Artificial Intelligence into Business

Sharad Gandhi

Christian Ehl

AI&U – Translating Artificial Intelligence into Business

Other book by the same authors:

The Social Resource

Translating Social Media into Business

Copyright © 2017 Sharad Gandhi, Christian Ehl

All rights reserved.

ISBN: 9781521717202

Dedication

We dedicate this book to **Computers, the Internet, and the Smartphone**. They have all developed during our careers to become the most powerful tools, transforming the world, and bringing enormous progress for humanity. They have set up the foundation for the next tidal wave of digital technologies we are about to experience.

Christian Ehl & Sharad Gandhi

Artificial Intelligence - CEO Perspective

"Artificial Intelligence is an amazing renaissance to technology, business and society. Machine Learning ... will empower and improve every business, every government organization, every philanthropy ... basically, there is not an institution in the world that cannot be improved with Machine Learning."

- **Jeff Bezos, CEO and Founder, Amazon**

"In an 'AI first' world we are rethinking all our products and applying Machine Learning and AI to solve user problems. We are doing that across every one of our products."

- **Sundar Pichai, CEO Google**

"Artificial intelligence is the 'ultimate breakthrough'. If I broadly talk about AI including machine learning, the thing that's been most exciting in the last five years is this one specialized branch of 'deep neural network' that is fundamentally giving us human perception, whether it is speech or image recognition, and that's just magical to see."

- **Satya Nadella, CEO Microsoft**

"AI is the next platform. All future applications, all future capabilities for all companies will be built on AI."

- **Marc Benioff, CEO Salesforce.com**

"I see an AI first world....I think very strongly that intelligent applications will fundamentally change the way you do work in the enterprise and the way you collaborate with your trading partners outside of the enterprise."

- **Bill McDermott, CEO SAP**

"Artificial intelligence is the key to the digital future of the Volkswagen Group"

- **Martin Hofmann, CIO Volkswagen**

"Success in creating AI could be the biggest event in the history of our civilization."

- **Stephen Hawking, Astrophysicist, Futurist**

"In the next 10 to 20 years, AI is going to be "extremely helpful" in managing our lives….The risk of artificial intelligence software becoming super smart is way out in the future"

- **Bill Gates, Philanthropist, Founder Microsoft**

Contents

Acknowledgments   9

Introduction   11
- Why Write This Book?
  - Our Goal: Demystify AI and its Adoption for Business
- What is This Book About?
  - Artificial Intelligence - the Next Big Thing
  - Some Clarification Upfront
- An Example of AI in Action
  - Skin Cancer Diagnosis Using AI

Part 1 – Understanding AI

1. What is Artificial Intelligence (AI)?   21
   - Alan Turing the Father of AI
   - Is Your Personal Computer Intelligent?
   - Algorithms - the Key to Intelligence
   - AI Automates Decision-Making
   - AI and Robots
   - Types of AI
   - Living with AI
   - AI - the Invisible Helper

2. Evolution of AI - How Did We Get Here?   33
   - A Brief History of Artificial Intelligence

3. How do AI Machines Learn? - Just Like Humans   39
   - How do Humans Learn?
     - Directed Learning
     - Assisted Learning (a.k.a. Supervised Learning)
     - Self-Learning (a.k.a. Unsupervised Learning)
   - Machine Learning (ML)
   - Deep Learning - the Magic of AI
   - AI System = Expert in a Black-Box
   - Building a Neural Network

4. Putting AI to Action   53

- AI Boosts Better Decision Making
- Duality of Intelligence for Decision Making
- Use of AI in Business

5. Role of AI in Technology   67

6. Role of AI in Business   75

7. Part 1 Concluding Remarks   77

Part 2: Leveraging AI for Your Business

Introduction   81

8. Why Now? AI - The Critical Ingredient   83
   - Quotes: Google, Salesforce, IBM, ... (AI First approach)
   - AI Use Cases (what's being done and available as modules)
   - Opportunity to Reinvent Your Business

9. AI Case Studies   93
   - Tesla Autonomous Vehicles/Mobility (diverse areas)
   - Salesforce.com (Einstein)
   - H&R Block Tax Consulting (IBM Watson)

10. Discovering Your AI Opportunity   103
    - Evolutionary Path - Enhance Existing Products
    - Radical Path - Disrupt Existing Solutions

11. Introducing the AI&U Canvas - Your AI Strategy Blueprint   123

12. Developing Your AI Strategy   129
    - Your AI&U Canvas
    - New Skills and Competencies
    - Organization - With a Data and AI Mindset

13. AI Outlook   135
    - Potential AI Scenarios
    - Challenges and Solutions for Workplace and Society
    - Right Balance Between Machines and Humans

Conclusions 139

Appendix

Sources and Recommended Reading 145

AI&U Workshops 151

About the Authors 153

Acknowledgments

Writing this book has been a truly eye-opening experience. We learned much from our discussions, research, engaging workshops, development of solutions and feedback from experts across the globe. We have come to truly appreciate artificial intelligence and the potential it has for a better future.

This book would not have been possible without the great encouragement of many people along the way. Thank you all for your motivation and support.

Special thanks goes to:

- **Manuela Ruf,** Sharad's girlfriend, for being an excellent sounding board and critique for our concepts to ensure ease of understanding for our non-technical audience.

- **Prakash Gandhi,** Sharad's father, who at the age of 97, has encouraged me by his interest in understanding the basic concepts of AI and related technology.

- **Lisa Ehl,** Christian's loving wife, for constantly reminding us to not let the bots take over.

- **Philip and Vincent Ehl,** Christian's children, whose generation will have to ensure that artificial intelligence will be used in a positive way for humanity and our planet.

Shannon Aziz has been a great help in tirelessly correcting and converting our writings into proper English, since both of us are non-native speakers. She has also helped us to get organized and coordinated all graphics and the publishing process. Thanks also to the graphics team at Hillert und Co., esp. **Maral Mihankhah,** who converted all our sketches into artwork which has helped greatly in easier understanding of our concepts and **Roen Branham,** who created the online version of this book.

It is great to be surrounded by so many intelligent people.

Sharad Gandhi & Christian Ehl

Introduction

As a child, I loved being called intelligent. It made me feel recognized as someone who could do wonders. Intelligence has always been seen as a uniquely human characteristic - a differentiating asset that sets us apart from all other animals. At times, we are generously willing to include certain animals like dolphins, chimpanzees, and dogs as intelligent. However, until recently, we have not regarded a machine as intelligent. We associate the word intelligence with our unique ability to learn, make decisions, and solve complex problems. We know from our experience that intelligent people are valued for their creative problem solving expertise and paid top salaries in most organizations.

Just a few short years ago, artificially created intelligence was regarded as impossible but today it is dramatically altering our lives. If intelligence can be artificially created then what has changed? During the industrial revolution, machines were invented to outsource human (and animal) physical and muscular power so that we humans were relieved of physical labor. Will artificially intelligent machines relieve humans in our thinking and decision-making capacity – to what extent and in what areas? What does it mean for individuals, our society, and future? These are intriguing and challenging questions with answers that are even more fascinating.

We believe that Artificial Intelligence (AI) is the most profound innovation by humans, with a far deeper and wider impact on our lives, than all preceding innovations from the steam engine of 1712 to the Internet. AI has the potential to transform the very role of humans in our society. As a result, it is extremely important for everyone, especially for business decision makers, to understand the power, significance, and relevance that AI will have not only on our lives but also on business and society as a whole.

Our Goal:
Demystify AI and Enable its Adoption for Business

AI is arguably one of the most popular technology topics of our time. Open a newspaper, switch on your television, it is a topic flooding every medium from popular to technical to social and political. It captivates the imagination, fantasies, and emotions of all. In spite of so much information, there is a need for clarity around the name and basic concepts of AI, possibly due to the ambiguity raised by media hype, differing definitions, technical jargon, and outrageous projections by science fiction. Our objective for writing this book is to demystify AI and its use so that it is understandable for a wide audience. We believe that with AI, industries and businesses have a tremendous opportunity to innovate, differentiate and deliver unique customer benefits.

What is this Book About?

A number of large companies like Google, Amazon, Facebook, Apple, IBM, Microsoft, Tesla, Alibaba, Tencent, Baidu, together with 1000s of innovative startups worldwide, are working tirelessly to develop the potential of AI and to offer the resulting benefits to businesses and customers. Their work is off the back of many years of groundbreaking AI research in universities and institutions around the world. Its progress and disruptive power is already, evident in a number of areas, from asking Siri to send a message to your spouse to autonomous driving. AI is radically transforming speech recognition, translation, spam mail detection, healthcare, and autonomous vehicles. AI is inevitable and will very soon become mainstream. The use of AI for future competitiveness and survival is becoming a must. Building AI focused products and services can and must start now. Those companies that took early advantage of digital technologies—like Sony cameras—have thrived, and those which did not—like Kodak—have perished. For most traditional businesses, developing and finalizing a robust business value proposition and a business model based on a new opportunity like AI is a challenging and difficult process. It often requires bold decision-making from top-level management since a number of organizational changes and Change Management are needed to transform a company from the status quo to one that is prepared for the future with a new business model based on new technologies.

Artificial Intelligence - the Next Big Thing

AI is projected to have a disruptive and transformational impact on businesses and industries. Unlike standard computers, AI systems have the ability to learn from historical cases, tuning themselves with every case to improve their accuracy in making better predictions and decisions. Like us humans, they can learn from experience. Initially, AI's most valuable and largest contribution will come from its ability to automate decision-making from provided inputs e.g. automatically and accurately determining all objects in a given image, or figuring out if an insurance claim is a fraud. Making better decisions is the key to success and AI can decrease the cost of making better decisions in many situations. This is likely to have a major impact on the way products and services are being designed, manufactured and sold. It will create new jobs and opportunities, but also make many traditional ones obsolete thus transforming industries and lifestyles.

Through this book, we are sharing our insights on what AI is, how it works, and what it can do for you. Our focus is on simplification of key concepts and articulating the unique benefits of AI. Since AI offers very significant opportunities to innovate, we wish to motivate you to start applying it in the development of your upcoming products, services, and business processes.

Some Clarifications Upfront

We would like to clarify a few points upfront:

- Most AI applications today, and in the very near future, apply to narrow and specific areas like recognizing objects in an image, speech recognition and text translation. In contrast, human intelligence applies to a very vast area. AI technology will take several decades to achieve the breadth and depth of human intelligence.

- AI today is not perfect and cannot deliver 100% error-free outputs. As we all know, nothing is error free, not even human predictions and decisions. However, the performance of (narrow) AI systems is superior and more accurate than that of us normal people, making it attractive in many applications. In the initial phase of deployment, AI decisions will be applied as expert opinions or guidance. Final decision to take action can still be taken under human supervision following the AI recommendation. At some point in the future, when a high trust in AI decision is established, the human approval will most likely be seen as redundant and dropped.

- In assessing errors and mistakes in performance, we are much more tolerant to mistakes made by humans, caused by forgetfulness, being tired, being distracted, falling asleep etc. However, we expect AI machines to be perfect and error-free. Eventually we will recognize that machines make far fewer mistakes than an average human, are cheaper, and easier to maintain. That will tip the balance in favor of AI solutions.

- Every technology can be used and abused. AI delivers significant benefits and innovations for almost all industries. However, we are aware that a powerful technology like AI can also be used to do harm. Science fiction often paints many negative scenarios of how AI will dominate the world, exploiting and subjugating humans to menial and degrading roles. Much more concerning is the imminent issue of job displacement, retraining, and unemployment of those who lose jobs to AI and robots in the very near future. As a consequence and number of other problems can arise, like growing inequality, social tensions, and geopolitical shifts. Unfortunately, at the time of writing, we have not come across any satisfying solutions for these issues.

The first section of this book focuses on making AI understandable, providing an easy to understand background on some fundamental questions: What is AI? What does it really do? How does it work? How did it evolve? How can machines be made intelligent? How do they learn? How does it fit with other digital technologies? What makes it useful in business?

The second section is focused on putting AI into action for your business - in an evolutionary as well as in a disruptive fashion. By using a few case studies we illustrate how AI is being used to create customer and business value. What skills and competencies are needed, how to develop or acquire them, and how to integrate AI into a product or process? We explore some issues like the role of humans in the future of collaborative work with AI, the future of work in the society, and the social consequences of the AI revolution. Lastly, we seek to address the outlook - what is the end game and where are we heading?

An Example of AI in Action – Skin Cancer Diagnosis Using AI

Let us illustrate some unique qualities and benefits of AI with an example.

Could a machine distinguish skin cancer from a benign skin condition—acne, a rash, or a mole—by simply scanning a photograph? Can a machine do it as accurately as an expert dermatologist, or even better? A research group at the Stanford University set out to find out the answers.

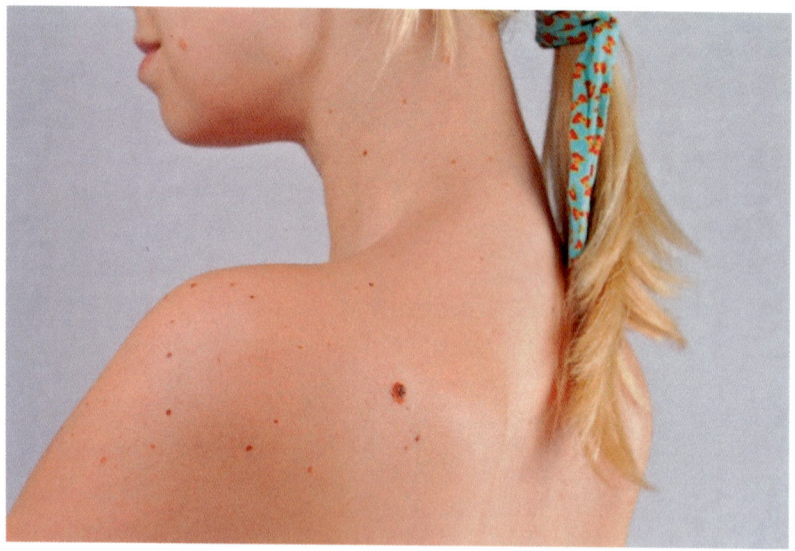

Computer scientists at Stanford have created an AI diagnosis algorithm for skin cancer

Stanford researchers started with an existing deep learning algorithm for AI built by Google for image classification. Just like any dermatologist, an AI system has to be trained to become accurate at diagnosing skin cancer. In order to do this the Stanford researchers used a "teaching-set" of 13,000 validated image samples spanning 2,032 different diseases, where each image had been diagnosed and thus categorized by dermatologists as benign lesions, malignant lesions, or non-cancerous growths. The deep neural network of the AI system then scanned these images pixel by pixel, looking for the characteristics common to each diagnosis. The AI system learned to diagnose these images and compared its diagnosis with the "correct" answer provided by the dermatologists. Subsequently, then, based on how accurate it was, the AI system tuned itself with every sample to improve its accuracy for the next diagnosis. After iteratively learning by comparing its diagnosis with that diagnosed by dermatologists through the vast number of images, its diagnosis became as accurate as the best dermatologists. In a side-by-side comparison, using 2000 gold standard test set of images, the AI system outperformed expert dermatologists.

The training and tests were done with high-quality images. With this said, more work needs to be done to make the system work with images taken with a smartphone and via the Internet for the diagnosis. Skin cancer diagnosis done by AI system with smartphone images could have an immense impact on the cost savings and value for patients and cost savings. Each year, some 5.4 million new cases of skin cancer are diagnosed in the United States. The usual process for identifying the many varieties of the disease involve a visual examination of moles or other marks on the skin by a dermatologist. In cases of doubt, a biopsy is needed. Early detection greatly increases the chances of survival - a five-year survival rate for melanoma detected early on is around 97 percent; but when detected in its later stages, that figure falls to around 14 percent.

This example illustrates the power of using AI for medical diagnosis. The use of images and patterns is very common in monitoring and diagnosis of many diseases. A well trained deep learning AI is excellent at extracting information from images, videos and patterns to accurately make the right decisions. A number of companies are very active in using AI for diagnosis. IBM Watson, an IBM supercomputer that combines artificial intelligence (AI) and sophisticated analytical software for optimal performance as a "question answering" machine, has made major progress with AI in diagnosing cancer and health disorders. We believe that AI will play a significant role in medical diagnosis for a wide range of diseases - lowering cost, reducing the time to detect, and saving lives.

Part 1 – Understanding AI

1. What is Artificial Intelligence?

Artificial Intelligence is often called by other names like Machine Intelligence, Machine Cognition, or Augmented Intelligence. They all have the same meaning.

First, let us start at a most basic level by simply defining Artificial Intelligence. Many have offered their perspective, however as of yet, no universally accepted definition exists. To illustrate the opinions, here are some examples:

"AI is the science and engineering of making intelligent machines, especially intelligent computer programs."

- **John McCarthy** (who coined the term Artificial Intelligence in 1956), Stanford University

"Artificial intelligence (AI) is the ability of a digital computer or computer-controlled robot to perform tasks commonly associated with intelligent beings. The term is frequently applied to .... intellectual processes characteristic of humans, such as the ability to reason, discover meaning, generalize, or learn from past experience."

- **Encyclopaedia Britannica**

AI is an area of computer science that deals with giving machines the ability to seem like they have human intelligence - the power of a machine to copy intelligent human behavior."

- **Merriam-Webster Dictionary**

We prefer the simplest definition of AI from Wikipedia:

"Artificial Intelligence (AI) is intelligence exhibited by machines."

While this may sound somewhat primitive it cuts to the core and recognizes the fundamentals. AI consists of two words: Artificial and Intelligence. The term "Intelligence" describes the cognitive function of humans (and animals) of becoming aware of situations, learning from them, and applying the learning to make decisions and to solve new problems. It includes one's capacity for logic, understanding, self-awareness, learning, emotional knowledge, planning, creativity, and problem-solving. We generally assume that a person of superior intellect can perform all these functions quickly and for a wide variety of situations and problems.

Colloquially, the term "artificial intelligence" is used when a machine mimics human "cognitive" functions associated with human brain, such as "learning" and "problem-solving". Our brain—with over 100 billion neurons, each connected to several thousand other neurons, making over 100-1000 trillion neural connections—is the most complex object in the known universe. Cognition is one of its most complex and advanced skills. Cognition is the mental action or process of acquiring knowledge and understanding through thought, experience, and senses, often for decision-making and problem-solving. Professor Linda Gottfredson (University of Delaware) puts it very well: "Cognition is the ability to learn, and learn from experience, think abstractly, comprehend complex ideas, reason, plan and solve problems."

In this way, human intelligence is not a single ability or cognitive process, but rather an array of separate components. Current AI focuses chiefly on a few components of intelligence: learning, reasoning, problem-solving, perception, and understanding language.

Alan Turing - the Father of AI

If you ask any AI specialist who the "Father of AI" is they will readily say "Alan Turing, of course!" Others may recall his story pictured beautifully in the 2014 movie "The Imitation Game" portraying the nail-biting race against time by Turing and his team cracking the Nazi Enigma code during the darkest days of World War II.

During the Second World War, Alan Turing built one of the first computers. It had just one goal: to crack the secret Nazi code for their submarine attacks on ships of the British and Allies in the Atlantic Ocean. Turing played a pivotal role in cracking intercepted coded messages that enabled the Allies to defeat the Nazis in many crucial engagements and in doing so helped win the war. It has been estimated that this work shortened the war in Europe by more than two years and saved over fourteen million lives.

Fig. 1.1 Alan M. Turing, considered to be the father of Artificial Intelligence

Turing is widely considered to be the father of theoretical computer science and artificial intelligence. In 1950 Alan Turing published his famous paper, popularly called the "The Imitation Game." He started with the basic question, "Can machines think?" By discarding traditional means of answering this he developed the 'Turing Test' as the best way to determine if a machine can successfully imitate a human thinker. Turing put forward the idea of an 'imitation game', in which a human being and a computer would be interrogated under conditions, where the interrogator would not know which was which, the communication being entirely by textual messages. Turing argued that if the interrogator could not distinguish them by questioning, then it would be unreasonable not to call the computer intelligent, because we judge other people's intelligence from external observation in just this way.

Later in the paper, he expands the basic AI question "Can machines think?" to "Can a machine learn?", linking the ability to independently think to the ability to learn. If a machine can learn, what is the best way to teach a machine? One of his propositions is precisely what has become successfully adopted today as "deep learning". In his words, "This process could follow the normal teaching of a child. Things would be pointed out and named". The machine, like a child, can be taught by examples. The more variation of examples, the better the learning and subsequently better are the decisions the machines makes.

Is Your Personal Computer Intelligent?

Many household gadgets like washing machines, dishwashers, air conditioners, and even personal computers seem intelligent in the sense that they automatically perform complex logical tasks. But are they really intelligent? Some say no. Even if we were to classify them as intelligent, their intelligence is "programmed intelligence"— as the intelligence does not originate within the machine, but human developers have programmed it into the machine. Humans have created the algorithms (the logic and sequence of steps) that allow these machines to exhibit intelligence. Many industrial robots performing complex tasks like welding and assembly in a factory are also run on algorithms programmed by humans.

Algorithms — the Key to Intelligence

It is these algorithms that play an important role in exhibiting intelligence. Algorithms are not only pertinent to machines but we humans also execute algorithms in our brain when we decide to buy Google stock vs. Microsoft's, or going on vacation to Mallorca vs. the Bahamas. Every person develops their unique algorithms for dealing with life situations through their subjective learning and life experiences — that is why we often make different decisions when faced with a similar choice of options. However, in contrast to algorithms programmed by humans in a machine, Artificial Intelligence (AI) is capable of creating its own algorithms through the process of "machine learning" and making decisions based on the self-developed algorithms — similar to humans. Learning, creating and optimizing its own algorithms is the unique characteristic of AI.

AI Automates Decision-Making

Functionally, AI is an automated decision-making system for a specific area of expertise, such as, healthcare, taxation, investment, translation, speech recognition, or face detection. AI deduces the best answer or decision (with the highest probability of success) for any given new situation within the context of its expertise.

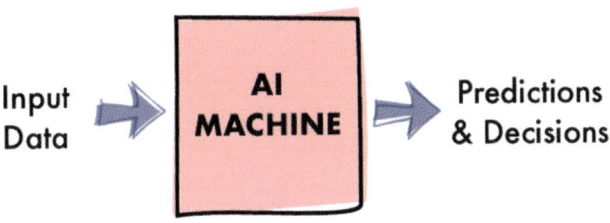

Fig. 1.2 AI is an automated decision-making system for a specific area of expertise

Making better decisions is the key to success in not only business but also in our personal life. Artificial Intelligence is rapidly decreasing the cost and time for making better decisions in all walks of life. The decision making skill of AI allows it to perform even complex operations like identifying multiple objects in an image, summarizing the happenings in a video clip, scene understanding, and figuring out the next steps in a game.

AI and Robots

People often confuse robots with AI. While the two are related they are distinct. A robot is a machine that sometimes mimics the human in some activity, but the AI itself is the algorithmic logic inside the robot. AI is the brain, and the robot is its body. Robotics face two challenges: physical and logical. Physical: to make the physical body behave and move as required for the desired activity. Logical: the AI part (the robot brain) must figure out and decide what to do as a response to new inputs and situations. Another misplaced belief about robots is that they are designed as look-alike human-ersatz. Most industrial robots look anything but human and are designed for a very specific task. Their shape, form, and capabilities are optimized for that specific task - like welding, assembly or moving heavy objects. They look anything but human. Science fiction movies and some consumer products make robots look like a human, more in an iconic sense. In most such movies they show that destroying the robot body does not kill the robot, one has to defeat the AI within that runs the robot. An interesting version of dealing with a misbehaving robot is pictured in the over 50 year old classic science fiction "2001: A Space Odyssey." HAL is the AI and the entire spaceship is the robotic body managed by HAL. When human astronauts believe that HAL is misbehaving and has gone rogue, their only option is to switch off the computer running HAL to regain control of the spaceship.

Furthermore, AI does not require a physical body to express itself. AI can be viewed as an information processing black box containing the specialized learned cognition. Input is a stream of data representing a new situation or a query. The output is the information for decision support or a desired action. Here are a few examples of AI enhanced information services to illustrate that AI needs no physical body:

AI Application	Input Data	Learned Cognition	Output / Decision
Apple Siri – Speech Amazon Alexa Google Assistant	Spoken query	Speech recognition algorithms and contextual information	Response – queried information or action
IBM Watson Healthcare for cancer	Patient data and history	Cancer diagnosis cases and research. Treatment success rates	Diagnosis and treatment recommendation
Income tax AI	Taxpayer's financial information	Tax laws, past cases, risk assessments	Income tax submission recommendations with best returns
Traffic routing	Start and destination. Traffic and road situation	Prediction of traffic development and delays	Best route to destination with information and options
Spam filtering	New email	History and patterns of spams. User profile	Spam or no-spam
Product recommendation	New product selection, user profile and shopping history	History of products bought and what else was bought, or makes sense	Focused recommendation with most relevance in the context of product selected

Fig. 1.3 AI enhanced information services illustrating that AI needs no physical body

Types of AI

The basic concepts of AI have not changed much since Alan Turing's time, however the approach to achieving it has. Significant progress has been made in the last 5–10 years due to advances in machine learning and deep neural networks, leading to a range of services (some shown above) that we all can readily experience today. Like any other technology, AI will evolve from addressing simple tasks to vastly more complex problems. The evolution of AI is commonly modeled in 3 stages. We are currently at the very beginning of the first stage.

1. **Artificial Narrow Intelligence (ANI):** In this stage, AI is focused on one specific area like translation, face recognition, playing chess or diagnosing cancer. Here the AI has been trained to support decision-making in one, and only one, area. An image recognition AI would have no clue about a game of chess. ANI could be compared to hiring a top specialist for doing just one job better than anyone else—but is fairly useless for any other tasks. Currently (2017), all AI applications are at the ANI stage. In the next 3–5 years, many new products and services will integrate ANI features offering unique customer value, creating a huge business opportunity for differentiation.

2. **Artificial General Intelligence (AGI):** The next stage is AGI, where the AI system is as intelligent as humans across the board performing any intellectual task that a human being can at a comparable level of expertise. An adult human acquires an abundance of knowledge and variety of skills and is capable of using all these in many combinations. Matching this is a lot bigger challenge than achieving expertise in one area. As of yet, no one has achieved creating an AGI. Average prediction by AI experts for achieving AGI is around the middle of this century. More optimistic predictions are by the year 2030. "When Will AI Exceed Human Performance? Evidence from AI Experts (https://arxiv.org/pdf/1705.08807v1.pdf)"

3. **Artificial Super-Intelligence (ASI):** AI expert Nick Bostrom defines Super-intelligence as "an intellect that is much smarter than the best human brains in practically every field, including scientific creativity, general wisdom, and social skills." Much better can mean anything - 10x, 1000x, or 1000000x. It is humanly impossible to imagine it, and even more, its impact on our lives and society. Experts prediction for achieving ASI is sometime in the second half of this century. When intelligent machines themselves start designing their next generation versions, progress becomes exponential and unimaginably fast. ASI is the stuff of science fiction at the moment.

Currently, and for the next few decades, all AI will be in the narrow segment (ANI). With this said, we should not underestimate what can be achieved by combining various automated AI decisions for a business solution. As an example, if video streams from all surveillance cameras in a public place are fed into a machine learning AI system, over time the system is able to establish the pattern of video data for a normal situation by itself. The system can then detect an exceptional situation based on the shifting patterns in the video feeds. Thus, based on the situation it is able to recommend the best action based on previous situations and decisions.

In this book, we will focus entirely on ANI technology and applications because it offers vast and immediate opportunities for business innovation in almost all industries. AGI and ASI are way beyond the scope of most businesses in this decade.

Living with AI

In the last two decades, the Internet and smartphones have become increasingly integrated into our lives—having crept in, almost unnoticed, bringing significant benefits. We realize the enormous change they have created only when we look back and reflect. Similarly, AI will creep into our lives transforming our businesses and lifestyle in ways that we cannot yet imagine. It is important to remember that AI is not a human substitute but an excellent teammate with complementing skills. Humans and AI will learn to collaborate as teammates—each bringing their unique skills to create a winning combination.

Skills – Humans excel at	Skills – AI excels at
Common sense	Pattern identification
Imagination and dreaming	Endless and tireless capacity
Abstraction	Natural language
Generalization	Locating knowledge
Dilemma	Machine learning
Ethics and morals	Eliminating bias

Fig. 1.4 AI complements human skills

Jack Ma, Chairman, and CEO of Alibaba, the world's largest retailer, points out that artificial intelligence technologies are essential for humanity, but ultimately machines should not replace people. According to the entrepreneur, the technological community should prioritize developing solutions to make the robots do only what people can't do. Thus, robots can become "human partners", not opponents. He goes one further to even predicting the emergence of a Robot-CEO, "In 30 years on the cover of Time, as the best CEO of the year, we will probably see a robot; he remembers better than us, he considers us better than us, and will not argue with his competitors"

AI - the Invisible Helper

Technology has forced humans to learn several new and "unnatural" skills. In the last 50 years alone we have had to learn to input information by typing on a keyboard (instead of speaking, or hand-writing),to read and use information on a screen (instead of paper), to use a mouse for navigation and actions (instead of gestures), and to using touch screens for interacting with computing and communication devices. In order to navigate through information we learned scrolling, clicking, panning, and zooming with multiple windows and apps. In hindsight, it is easy to dismiss these skills as trivial. In reality, we needed to practice, to learn, to master and incorporate them into our daily lives. They come easy to some us, but not for all. The good news is that AI will not require us to learn new skills —instead, AI will allow us to revert to using some of our natural and fundamental human skills and make interactions easier and intuitive. AI is becoming the invisible helper in our lives.

As the invisible helper, understanding natural human speech is extremely helpful. AI has almost perfected the understanding of speech, recognizing not just what we speak but also the correct context. Any of us can experience using this today via Apple Siri, Amazon Alexa, or Google Assistant. The performance will only improve over time and become as accurate in understanding as another human being—perhaps even more so as computers do not get distracted, tired, or subjective in capturing what is spoken. Other areas that are also being perfected by AI are recognizing and interpreting facial expression, gestures, images, and objects. In addition, the quality of language translation between many commonly used languages may not yet be perfect but has reached better than average human levels. The same is true for text to speech conversion. Eventually, by combining all these, we will be able to interact via speech with anyone, in any language and with any device, in the world. With speech and gesture interface, our interaction with devices will be simplified significantly —meaning no confusing buttons, icons, and screens to navigate. Just say what you want and AI takes care of the rest, making speech the new human interface. This will also open up the market to a much larger section of society for products and services —especially to those who feel intimidated and overwhelmed by computer technology and its interfaces.

At an even higher level, AI will be able to link many devices and services needed to cater to our complex need, making it unnecessary to understand and remember individual steps. If for example you felt like watching a Star Wars episode on a Friday night, the mere command "Show me the latest Star Wars movie" is all you would need. AI would listen and take all the necessary steps: switch on the TV and other devices —to your preferred settings, search for which is the latest Star War movie, compare providers with the best offers (Netflix, Amazon etc.), purchase, set room lighting, start movie streaming and say, "Enjoy the movie, The Last Jedi." Speech AI makes interacting with multiple devices and services so easy. It clearly sets course for personal AI Bots, who know you and your preferences.

AI, by itself, will not be a new product or service. It is an ingredient technology that will be integrated invisibly into products, for enhanced ease of use and to deliver higher value to users. Many products and services we know and use today are already AI enabled —to name a few, Google Translate, Apple Siri, Amazon Recommendations. AI makes for a much more natural user experience all around; It is richer, personalized, and holistic —and suitable to a much broader audience. Many advantages of AI in products and services may not stand out as something new. These products will just appear to be much easier to use or just better as a result of AI.

In two simple sentences, Jeff Bezos, CEO of Amazon, summarized what most people need to understand about artificial intelligence and positioning its scope:

"Over the past decades, computers have broadly automated tasks that programmers could describe with clear rules and algorithms. Modern machine learning techniques now allow us to do the same for tasks where describing the precise rules is much harder."

He captures very well the invisible nature and "behind the scene" role of AI and machine learning as he elaborates on how it applies to Amazon: "Much of what we do with machine learning happens beneath the surface. Machine learning drives our algorithms for demand forecasting, product search ranking, product and deals recommendations, merchandising placements, fraud detection, translations, and much more. Though less visible, much of the impact of machine learning will be of this type — quietly but meaningfully improving core operations."

2. The Evolution of AI — How Did We Get Here?

When asked "What was your first experience with artificial intelligence?", most people call upon science fiction movies. Long before that though, there have been myths about artificial intelligence from ancient times, as well as hints in literature such as, Mary Shelley's Frankenstein. But early science fiction movies like Star Trek played on the themes of alien intelligence and machine intelligence. In modern time, these movies have inspired entire product generations. Today it has turned out that a surprising number of those concepts are actually feasible and many of them have made it into the mainstream. The mobile phone as a ubiquitous communicator, the full-body scanner, the space ships, autonomous flight objects, just to name a few. Often the products have an astonishing physical resemblance to those fantasies created in the movies that were envisioned by the authors.

Science fiction movies have created all kinds of artificial intelligence visions, both positive and negative. Unfortunately, with today's technological advancement, even the darkest visions have become imaginable. Various movie themes explore how the artificial intelligence takes control of the human race and begins to treat us in the same manner we treat animals. One movie, 'The Matrix', describes how an AI network called the Matrix virtually controls people's minds by playing a virtual world into their brains that humans perceive to be the real world. The Matrix AI reduces the role of humans to mere energy sources and are kept in cells to extract their energy while keeping them distracted by simulating a virtual world in their brains. The breadth of movies created are a proof of the amazing human creativity and showcase the fears that humans have for the unknown.

Fig. 2.1 The Matrix: An example of how AI is often shown in science fiction

My own first encounter with artificial intelligence was in programming in the early 80s. Being a technology fascinated child, I spent many evenings in front of the first computers at university, programming games and exchanging code on telephone-connected bulletin boards. We developed utility programs, such as address books and calendars, which did not exist as widely available computer programs at that time. We asked ourselves, how can we make it more intelligent? If we could ask them questions, could they answer? From there, we began to create a general purpose interface, where the computer would ask you what you would like to know. By engaging in a simple dialog, the computer could analyze the texts and respond with predefined answers, sometimes reusing the words that you had used in the question. The main logic was based on "if this, then that" and we made complex branches and calculations to make the computer feel intelligent to the program users. Coding intelligence was fun in the beginning, but eventually, we got frustrated by the sheer volume of code and the limits of the early machines. External users of our applications found our interface quite ineffective and rather unintelligent. Artificial Intelligence has a long history of great aspirations and many failures.

A Brief History of Artificial Intelligence

As mentioned previously, Alan Turing is considered the father of AI. His theory of computation suggested that a machine, by using 1s and 0s, could simulate mathematical operations, and shortly thereafter, could simulate any formal reasoning. At the same time, discoveries in neurology, information theory, and cybernetics led to the first concept of building an electronic brain. Around 1956, the field of AI research emerged at the Dartmouth conference with John McCarthy from Stanford University. The first artificial intelligence program, Logic Theorist, was born. This program mimicked the problem-solving capabilities of humans by focusing on pattern recognition. This initiated tremendous research in the field of AI, leading people to believe that within 20 years' time, machines would be capable of doing any work that people can do. At this time, various approaches were tested from programming knowledge into the computer to recognizing patterns through algorithms. Soon, progress slowed due to lack of tangible results, leading to an AI winter, causing funding of AI projects to dry up, further slowing the process to a near halt.

1950	Alan Turing published "Computing Machinery and Intelligence"
1955	The term "artificial intelligence" is coined by John McCarthy (Dartmouth College), Marvin Minsky (Harvard University), Nathaniel Rochester (IBM), and Claude Shannon (Bell Telephone Laboratories)
1955	Herbert Simon and Allen Newell develop the Logic Theorist, the first artificial intelligence program
1958	John McCarthy develops the programming language Lisp which becomes the most popular programming language used in artificial intelligence research

1997	Deep Blue becomes the first computer chess-playing program to beat a world chess champion
2011	IBM Watson, a natural language question answering computer, competes on Jeopardy and defeats two former champions
2016	Google DeepMind's AlphaGo defeats Go champion Lee Sedol

Fig. 2.2 A brief history of artificial intelligence

In the 1980s, AI research picked up again. Initial success of the so-called expert systems derived from emulating the decision making ability of humans, by extensively using if-then-else rules, acting on a growing pool of knowledge that was preloaded in the system, and then continuously expanded. Expert systems became the first commercial successes of artificial intelligence software.

However, public attention soon shifted towards the rising microcomputer, which put an end to early machines like the Lisp machine. The evolving new world of personal computing attracted most of the computing talent and caused a lack of attention on AI research. Soon a second AI winter arose, lasting until the early 1990s.

The personal computer was no solution in solving the challenges of artificial intelligence; with its standardized instruction sets, mostly serial in nature, the highly parallel nature of neural network computing advanced only slowly. However, the increasing graphics nature of personal computers, driven by ever realistic games full of special effects, demanded a highly parallel graphics chip architectures. New parallel architectures grew, ever decreasing in costs due to Moore's law.

Due to this increasing computational power, AI progressed and gained greater emphasis on solving specific problems often in areas of logistics, data mining and medical diagnosis. This so-called narrow AI benefited from the growing computing power and the availability of more research experts in the field of artificial intelligence.

An area that greatly altered the perceptions of the general public was gaming. For example, the competitive area of computer chess-playing, which funded further development of IBM's Deep Blue, becoming the first computer to beat the reigning world chess champion, Garry Kasparov on 11 May 1997. Thanks to advanced statistical techniques, large amounts of data being readily available, much faster computers as well as new machine learning techniques, AI continued to expand and flourish by the mid-2010s. Subsequently, IBM's Watson beat the two greatest Jeopardy champions, Brad Rutter and Ken Jennings by a significant margin and Google AlphaGo's won over world champion Lee Sedol in Go March 2016. People have since begun to accept that computers have made great advancements in artificial intelligence and a lot more is to be expected.

General public awareness has been stimulated and led to a general recognition of the inevitable evolution of AI. All of this was fuelled by events like the arrival of smart personal assistants on smartphones as well as success stories of AI progress, such as IBM's Watson being used to help diagnose cancer. This mental shift towards AI also had an impact on the financial investment market, which has continued to heat up since 2015. The recent availability of affordable neural networks has also helped speed up the development.

For the past few years, significant progress has been made in concrete areas of computer vision, image recognition, natural language processing, pattern recognition, knowledge location, and machine learning subsequently leading to ever more applications of artificial intelligence in real-world problems. Over 550 startups alone, using AI as a core part of their products, raised $5B in funding in 2016. All leading technology companies have built capable teams of several thousands of people focussing on AI, with the additions of top research talent from leading institutions, which were often hired into the company's teams. AI has become the hottest topic in the startup world, attracting the most funding for future oriented technologies in 2016.

The fast technological evolution of artificial intelligence in recent years will likely be the cause of a fundamental business transformation based on artificial intelligence. We are really only at the beginning. The transformation is fuelled by the impact of AI on software, the new capabilities in consumer products and the fast-paced advancement in robotics. The sheer scale of artificial intelligence investments, as well as the quickly growing number of people working in AI areas, lay the groundwork of a new economic revolution.

3. How AI Machines Learn? —Just Like Humans

Without learning there is no intelligence.
Without intelligence there is no learning.

Learning is the cumulative process of acquiring information, and developing skills to figure out how to solve new problems, and deal with new situations.

If learning is a prerequisite for intelligence then what is the prerequisite for learning? A rock or a plant cannot learn as it lacks this capacity. For humans and animals in general, thanks to the brain, we have the capacity to learn from our environment. Learning is critical to our survival. At birth, we possess a bootstrap set of knowledge for our basic survival needs. This resides in the limbic region—one of the innermost parts of the brain. Over millions of years of evolution, it has been programmed to provide us with our primal survival mechanisms and basic instincts. However, that alone is not enough. The larger part of the human brain, the cerebral cortex, with over 20 billion neurons, each connected to several thousand other neurons, is our neurally networked learning organ. It gives us our capacity to learn, to store our learning, make decisions, and to act. The large size and complexity of our brains make us the ultimate learning species on earth.

So the question is, how do we make all these neurons in our brain help us learn, acquire skills to solve new problems, and deal effectively with new ambiguous situations and uncertainty? Understanding the process of learning and decision-making in humans helps us discover techniques to make machines learn. So how do we humans learn? Here is a simplified view:

Learning is mostly about interpreting data patterns. The human brain is an incredible pattern-recognition machine. Our brains constantly process sensory inputs, label them as a dog, or a cake, and then generate a decision, or an action, as an 'output' (this dog is not dangerous, this cake looks delicious, I want to eat it). Our brain is a sophisticated pattern management system for recognizing, storing, and comparing data patterns. We constantly observe incoming data patterns and the resulting outcomes, and based on repeated observations our brain develops an algorithm of how data patterns correlate with outcomes. As we continue observing more and more patterns and the related outcomes, we improve our ability to deduce the right conclusion about what it means (prediction) and what needs to be done (decision). It must be pointed out that this is a statistical, and hence a probabilistic, process of arriving at conclusions — which is error prone. We occasionally do make mistakes and recognize a wolf for a dog, or a plastic look-alike for a delicious cake. Our algorithmic learning becomes more refined and we are able to see subtle differences in data patterns that produce a different outcome. That is why, practice makes us better (but never perfect) and experience counts. A medical doctor who has seen thousands of cases of heart problems is able to quickly read the pattern in the symptoms much better than a less experienced doctor. A professional tennis player, with thousands of hours of practice, can predict quite accurately where the ball is going to land, just by observing the body and action of the opponent as they serve.

In order to learn, machines must have the capacity to learn. They must have a pattern recognition and management system. In modern Artificial Intelligence systems with Machine Learning capabilities, this is provided by an artificial neural network. The neural network of an AI system is analogous to the neural network of the brain in a human. The concept of machine learning using neural networks for learning is not new, but due to recent advances in neural computing hardware, access to a large number of labeled data sets for AI training, and sophisticated deep learning techniques, machine learning and AI have now become a practical reality.

How do Humans Learn?

There are many techniques by which humans learn. They provide different ways of developing algorithms in the brain, which correlate input data patterns with outcomes. Here we illustrate three human learning techniques and show how they can translate into machine learning.

1. Directed Learning

This is a simple method of providing exact step-by-step instructions to perform a given task—with little scope for deviating from the prescribed procedure. This is typically used for training workers on traditional assembly lines to execute a specific task precisely and identically every time. The only learning that happens is on how to exactly follow a procedure. This technique does not provide any means to deal with situations for which no instructions are provided.

This is how most classic computer programs works. A program is essentially a precise sequence of steps which a computer must blindly execute—exactly as designed by a human programmer. Crashes occur when unforeseen situations happen, because the computer has never been taught how to deal with such a situation. First generation of AI systems were victims of this strictly logical approach. Human programmers had essentially codified their interpretation of all possible data patterns into an IF-THEN-ELSE logic, just like most computer programs are written. The AI machine itself was not capable of drawing its own conclusions as it had never really learned to deal with an un-programmed situation.

2. Assisted Learning (a.k.a. Supervised Learning)

This is how a good teacher teaches students. The focus of teaching is not just to learn the exact subject matter, but also to learn how to learn and to understand the general topic. Teaching is done using illustrative examples. The teacher teaches a topic using many typical examples or cases. This enables the student to self-develop the logic that connects the data input with its corresponding outcome in each example used. To learn how to recognize cats, a child is shown hundreds of pictures of cats, along with pictures of other objects and animals that may look like a cat, pointing out in each case which one is a cat and which is not. The children look at each picture and they themselves develop the algorithm for how to recognize a cat (with no instructions or descriptions provided). Similarly, a radiologist learns how to detect specific abnormal medical conditions (like a tumor) by studying a large number of labeled images. The radiologist develops their own algorithm to quickly detect an anomaly within seconds. This is how our brain learns. It is able to spot information encoded in data patterns and to convert it into conclusions and decisions. This ability becomes very focused and precise with increasing number and diversity of cases experienced, making the decision-making automatic and beyond thinking. This is real learning. Through more and more practice people can deal with most situations — however ambiguous or unpredictable — just through self-developed and trained algorithms. This is how we learn languages, mathematics, music, tennis, skiing etc. The instructor starts us off with illustrative cases, which provide data patterns and outcomes. Then our brain develops the necessary algorithm by observing the correlation between subtleties in data patterns and the respective outcomes, allowing us to deal with most new situations.

This way of learning is also how IBM Watson works. To make Watson the best expert at diagnosing cancer, it is fed millions of past cases of cancer; with details on symptoms, recommended treatments and observed outcomes. These cases provide Watson with patterns of symptoms and treatments leading to outcomes. In addition, it is also fed with all research papers on oncology—which provide additional patterns based on the latest worldwide understanding on diagnosis and treatments for cancer. The neural networks within Watson develop its generic algorithms based on the patterns in this massive amount of information. This is how it learns to diagnose cancer and recommend treatments. IBM Watson has become an immense help to the doctors in guiding them in medical decisions. Google uses a similar technique for automatic translation; Facebook for face recognition, Amazon for generating product recommendation. Thanks to machine learning, theses machines are able to recognize and understand subtle patterns in images, sounds, and body language much more consistently than humans.

3. Self-Learning (a.k.a. Unsupervised Learning)

As children we all have learned a lot just by observing other people. In traditional India, an enlightened teacher (a guru) taught his students not through words or instructions, but by assigning them tasks or roles which he thought would self-teach students in developing right insights and skills as the next step in their education and growth. Learning then becomes a discovery that is self-motivated and self-directed. It is based on one's own observations and conclusions without the teacher's bias.

A lot of learning happens without a teacher. By repeatedly observing an activity we figure out the correlation between what someone does and its outcome. For example, just by watching games like football/soccer we can learn how the game is played, what situations lead to a goal, or a foul, how a penalty corner is played etc. After watching hundreds of games we are then able to even predict various outcomes before they happen. This is because we have learned the patterns in the game that lead to a given outcome. Machines are not yet capable of any useful unsupervised learning, however it is one of the heavily researched areas waiting for a breakthrough.

Assisted learning is currently the most common approach to machine learning using deep learning techniques (to be described next). However, it needs a huge volume of labeled data sets —which are expensive to produce —to train the AI neural networks. In contrast, unlabeled data is readily available and cheap. Self-learning from free flowing unlabeled data is the next big challenge of AI.

Humans are often able to learn with very limited data - often a couple of examples help us to create the necessary algorithms in our brains. Maybe this a result of our evolution that has sharpened our learning process from limited data and made it very efficient. It has also been observed that it takes a smaller volume of training data to teach a machine learning system that has already been trained for some other tasks —possibly, because the previous learning helped in some way to master the new task quicker. This may mean that if we subjugated fresh neural networks to a "basic schooling" program, they may learn other tasks faster, just like humans. That would justify why we all go through lessons in music, mathematics, biology, history, languages etc. in school irrespective of what profession we eventually practice. It possibly primes our brains to learn everything else faster. This does give hope that machines will someday be able to learn new tasks from very limited data. Professor Andrew Blake, Research Director at the Alan Turing Institute in the UK says: "We now have to distinguish between two kinds of data — there's raw data and labelled data. [Labelled] data comes at a high price. Whereas the unlabeled data which is just your experience streaming in through your eyes as you run through the world… and somehow you still benefit from that, so there's this very interesting kind of partnership between the labelled data — which is not in great supply, and it's very expensive to get — and the unlabeled data which is copious and streaming in all the time. And so this is something which I think is going to be the big challenge for AI and machine learning in the next decade — how do we make the best use of a very limited supply of expensively labelled data?"

Machine Learning (ML)

ML represents a major breakthrough that has enabled AI to go mainstream. It is a technique for teaching machines how to learn to do something, as opposed to the traditional approach of teaching computers exactly how to do something, as in traditional computers. For recognizing animals in images, instead of finding unique visual characteristics and patterns from images of those animals and then programming the logic for each animal, ML involves feeding images of those animals to a learning framework and letting the AI machine figure out on its own the visual patterns and significant differences between images of different animals. Hence the machine learns by itself instead of being specifically programmed to do a unique task. The core architecture used in ML is an artificial neural network. Data inputs are fed to the neural network (pixels of animal images in the previous example). Mathematical transformations are performed within the neural network producing a decision as its output (which animal). The output decision is a transformation of the data input by the neural network. The output is essentially a metamorphosis of the input. A butterfly is a good analogy. A caterpillar creates a cocoon around it and at some stage a butterfly emerges. The cocoon is the "neural network" that transforms the caterpillar into a butterfly.

Neural networks are inspired by the neurons in our brain and the way they are interconnected. Our brain has about 100 billion neurons, interconnected with other neurons. In an AI neural network a neuron is modeled with a "perceptron" (graphic on the right side). The comparison between a real neuron and a perceptron is just for our understanding. In reality, a neuron network in our brain is far more complex than any model we can create. To have a detailed understanding of how all this works requires an excellent understanding of mathematics and neurobiology and is out of this book's scope. Our objective is to provide an insight into the principles of operation of how a machine is able to learn to take decisions. What follows now is an explanation of how these neural networks are built and how they work. It is semi-technical and some readers may want to skip it.

On the following page there is a model of a neuron and its mathematical analog, a perceptron. Artificial neural networks are huge networks of perceptrons, each built with a processor running the mathematical equations of the perceptron.

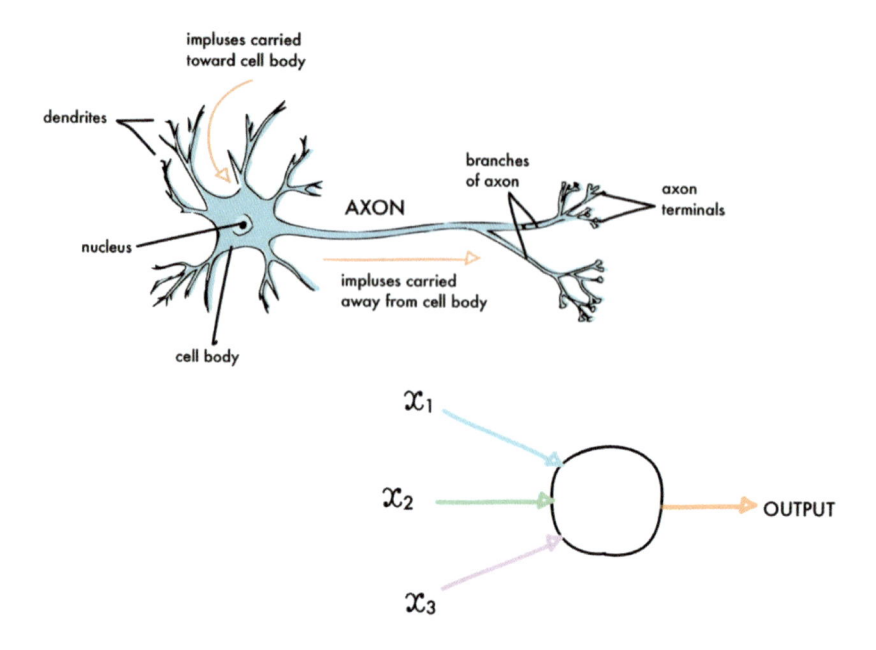

Fig. 3.1 A neuron and its mathematical analog, a perceptron

Each neuron has several impulse inputs called dendrites and one branching output called an axon. A transformation happens to the impulses within the neuron (and within the perceptron) between the inputs and the output. In the neuron, the transformation is electro-chemical; propagation is by means of a voltage difference called the action potential. The transformation in the perceptron can be represented by a mathematical function. The contribution of each input to the output is determined by the "weight" (w) associated with each input. The output carries a "bias" (b) and a non-linearity (or activation function). The perceptron with weights, bias, and the activation function is represented as follows:

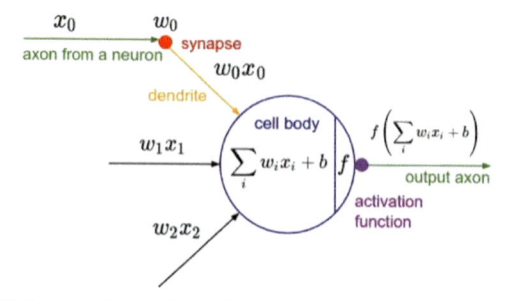

Fig. 3.2 Mathematical transformations within the neuron and a perceptron

The perceptron body transforms the inputs to a single output. This transformation depends on the weights, bias and the activation function.

In a neural network, thousands of perceptrons are networked together in multiple layers (depth) — creating a deep learning network.

Deep Learning — the Magic of AI

Deep learning is the magic behind the breakthrough success of ML in AI systems in this decade. It is this emerging area of computer science that offers the most promising approach for machine learning and it is revolutionizing artificial intelligence.

Deep learning requires a neural network having multiple layers — each layer doing mathematical transformations, and feeding into the next layer. The output from the last layer is the decision of the network for a given input. The layers between the input and output layer are called hidden layers.

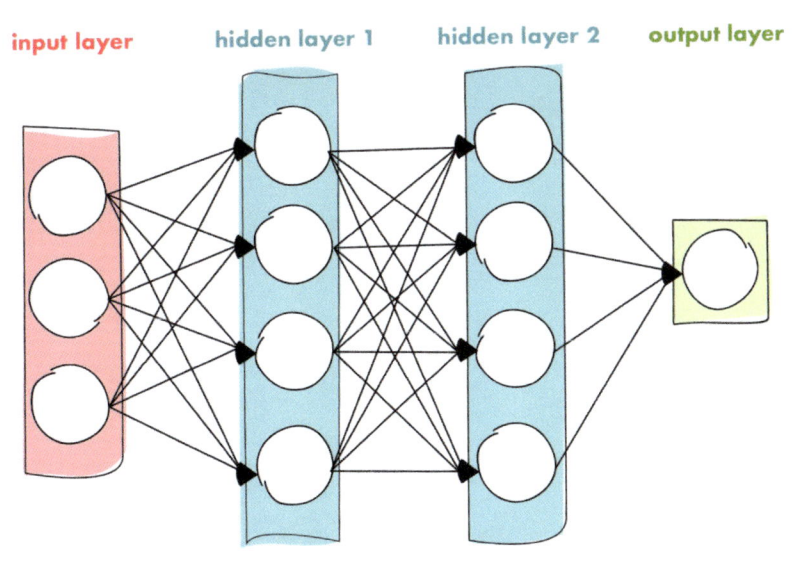

Fig. 3.3 Deep Learning — the magic of AI

A deep learning neural network is a massive collection of perceptron's interconnected in layers. The weights and bias of each perceptron in the network influence the nature of the output decision of the entire network. In a perfectly tuned neural network, all the values of weights and bias of all the perceptron are such that the output decision is always correct (as expected) for all possible inputs. How are the weights and bias configured? This happens iteratively during the training of the network — called deep learning.

Deep Learning Neural Network

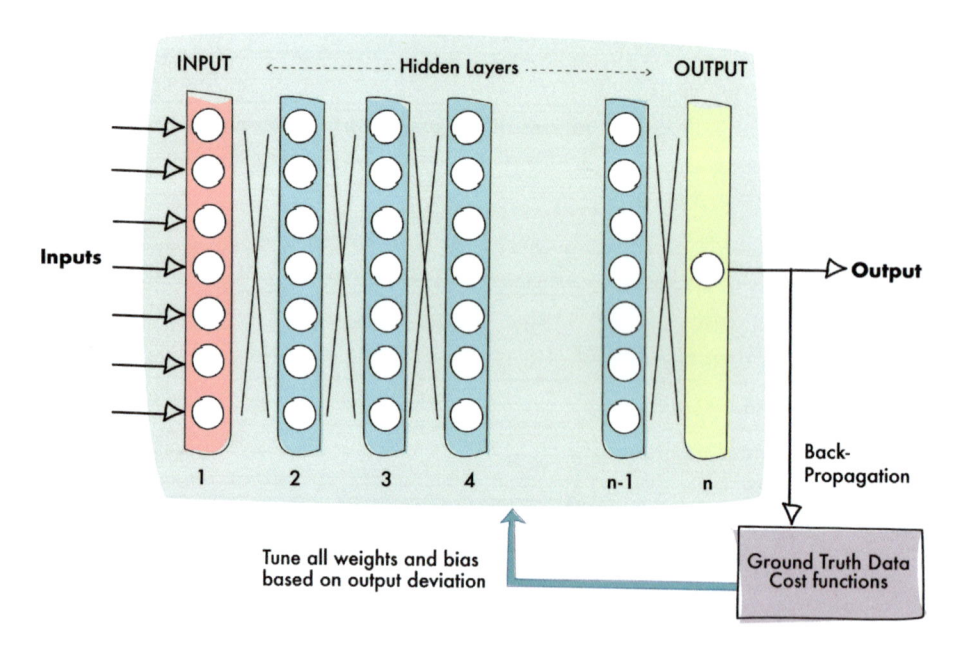

Fig. 3.4 Deep Learning within an artificial neural network

The diagram shows a deep neural network designed for deep learning with multiple layers. Data inputs enter the network into the input layer. Each layer has multiple perceptrons. They transform the inputs and generate outputs which feed into the inputs of the next layer. The interconnection between the layers and the mathematical function of each perceptron is determined by the deep learning network designers. The inputs get successively transformed layer by layer and eventually generate an output decision—a value between 0 and 1, indicating the confidence level (as a probability) of the decision for the input data. For example, if the input image is that of a cat and the network has to identify it as a cat, the confidence level should be as close as possible to 1. A lower value indicates that the network is not yet well optimized to identify the cat as a cat.

During the training phase of the neural network, the output is compared with the desired output. Deviations (errors) are back propagated through the network, adjusting and tuning the weights and biases of all the perceptrons in the network using the "cost function." Learning happens at every tuning of the network parameters. Training the network requires a vast number of cases where the desired output is known. At the conclusion of the training, all the weights and biases of all the perceptrons have been tuned to their final values, and the network is able to deliver the correct decision for all the cases. This is equivalent to having trained a specialist with lots of cases so that they have learned to take the correct decision in all situations. Now the neural network is ready for deployment.

The learning parameters are stored in the weights and biases of individual perceptrons in the network. A large number of perceptrons in the network results in a higher resolution in decision making — making them more valuable. Most neural networks have thousands of perceptrons. Modern neural networks are usually made up of approximately 10-20 layers and contain around 100 million programmable parameters. Since the algorithmic logic for decision making is spread out in the weights and biases of thousands of perceptrons, it is almost impossible to reconstruct the logic or rationale used for the decision making — making the AI system based on deep learning neural networks a black box.

Amazon CEO, Jeff Bezos says: "We are now solving problems with machine learning and artificial intelligence that were ... in the realm of science fiction for the last several decades. And natural language understanding, machine vision problems, it really is an amazing renaissance." Bezos calls AI an "enabling layer" that will "improve every business."

AI System = Expert in a Black-Box

Deep learning AI systems are "experts within a black box." They produce a decision for an input situation. The logic for generating the decision is not revealed. One cannot determine why it made that decision. It cannot explain why a text output is the best speech recognition for a given audio input or why a given diagnosis represents the most probable cause for inputs of symptoms and medical history.

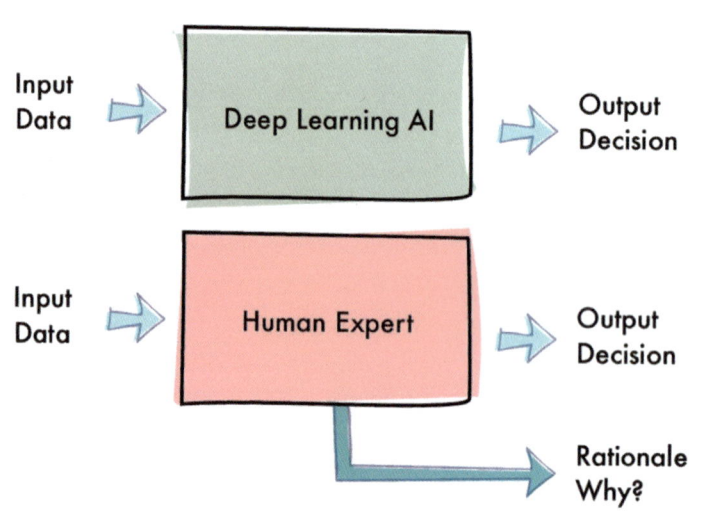

Fig. 3.5 Decision making — AI cannot provide a rationale for its decision, unlike a human expert

When we go to a human expert – a doctor, a tax consultant, or a financial advisor, we expect them to provide a rationale for the consultation advice or decision, which gives us confidence and trust in the advice offered. A deep learning AI system can provide us with the best advice and decisions, but does not, and cannot, provide the rationale for the decision. Deep learning technique that is used in AI systems cannot reveal the rationale used for decision-making. Just as we cannot understand the reasons behind perceptions and emotions of humans making decisions, we have to accept the opaqueness of AI systems, so long as we are happy with their decisions. Maybe a new technique will emerge to extract the rationale for an AI decision. Alternative methods of machine learning are being researched, where the rationale of decision is transparent—e.g. Bayesian method where you start with a hypothesis and every additional data input is used to tune that hypothesis.

Even if ML/AI decision-making remains a black box, there are significant advantages of leveraging AI for decision making. AI systems do not get distracted or tired, are generally more available, and they will get better and cheaper over time. AI systems can be exactly replicated and massively networked to work collaboratively with other AI systems. In contrast, the knowledge base and expertise of human experts has to develop individually and cannot be automatically networked. We believe that human experts and AI systems will work collaboratively, each contributing with their unique skills.

Data is the critical resource for machine learning. Patterns for learning and for taking decisions are contained in the data. Machine learning systems can produce valuable output if the data is relevant, clean, up-to-date, and reliable. In the new economy "data is the new oil" since AI converts data into business value.

Building a Neural Network

A neural network needs thousands of perceptrons. Each is a processor that executes the same function again and again with changing data. Thousands of simple processors with a very small instruction set are needed. This lies in the domain of HPC (High-Performance Supercomputers) with many processors running in parallel, which is very different from the software running on the processor in your personal computer or smartphone, which operates as a sequence of many instructions, needing a complex architecture. Interestingly, HPC architectures are also used in graphics processing in video games. As a result, Graphics Processing Unit (GPU) components (e.g. from NVidia), typically used in advanced video games consoles and PCs provided an excellent start in building fast, compact and low cost neural computing hardware. Now, dedicated hardware for deep learning neural networks have become the biggest rage in computer hardware, with many AI focused companies like Google, Facebook, IBM and Apple are building their own components for AI, along with traditional semiconductor companies like Intel, Qualcomm, and NVidia.

4. Putting AI to Action

Should I marry Susan or Karen, should I buy this house or that, should I take up this job or the other one, should I buy Google stock or Amazon, should I take a vacation this summer in Sicily or in Corsica, should I rent a BMW X5 or Audi Q5, should I take the highway or stay on the country roads to get to my destination faster.... Should I hire John or Sandra, should we partner with Microsoft or with Apple, should I outsource assembly to India or to China, should we target a broad customer base or focus on a special high margin segment? We are perpetually making decisions about a desired future outcome in all walks of our lives.

Making better decisions is the key to success—both in personal and in business life. A better decision means choosing the option that is considered the best from all angles, is the fastest, and the most accurate. As humans we have always tried to figure out the best way to arrive at a better decision. At the core, faced with uncertainty, decision-making is really about predicting the best option.

So how do we make better decisions? Most decisions were (are even now) made based on an amalgamation of personal experience, asking opinion of trusted friends, and gut feel. The emergence of digital technologies, especially the Internet, made decision-making more professional and easier—at least, at first. We now have unprecedented access to reports, opinions, research, comparisons, social media, and an expanse of additional data—allowing us to make data-based decisions. This is when it started becoming difficult again. The human brain has a fairly limited capacity for processing information from multiple inputs and becomes overwhelmed with too much data, resulting in decision-making paralysis. This is where many of us find ourselves today when we have to make a decision. Either we do not decide at all, or we decide based on just 3–5 factors (often ignoring the significant ones), or just surrender to our gut feel.

The benefit of data is that it provides objectivity in decision-making and forces us to look at various aspects and angles. However, too much of it overwhelms our decision-making abilities. There is much talk of being buried in data. For example, with thousands of new papers published on medical research every year, no medical professional can be expected to read and digest every new insight and use them in their daily job. It is not just a matter of available time, but also the capacity of our brain for inputs, actively using them, and making a sense of them for a decision. This is true for most professions—lawyers, tax consultants, and engineers. Is there a way to objectively make decisions, always factoring in all available information?

AI Boosts Better Decision Making

AI systems do not have the same limitations of our brain. AI can process millions of inputs, without ignoring a single one. And it can do so extremely fast, without rest, without tiring, without distraction, or becoming emotional. AI is an excellent complement to our brain in decision-making. AI is essentially a prediction machine, providing a fairly accurate prediction of the best outcome for a given input situation. Machine Learning has provided modern AI systems with the ability to self-learn from thousands of cases provided.

Anatomy of data based action

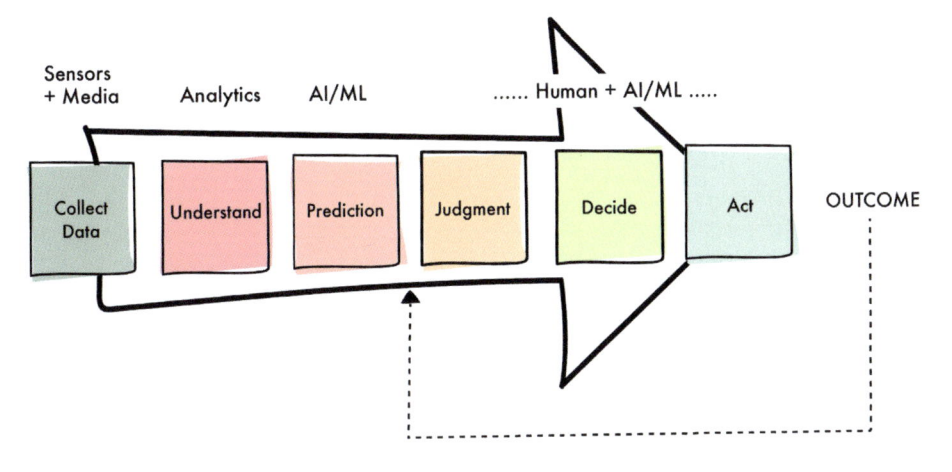

Fig. 4.1 Anatomy of data based decision making

Decision making starts with data inputs. Some systems use analytics to improve the understanding of the input before using AI. AI/ML generates a prediction in the form of a probability value for the best answer corresponding to the input. Based on the prediction a judgment has to be made to decide the best action. Judgment is a human skill that takes into account the prediction and any other considerations (like emotions, timing etc.). Action results from the decision. The consequences of the action are fed back into the system for tuning. For example, in a skin cancer diagnosis system, the input consists of medical data in form of medical images, reports, and medical history. Based on these the AI system gives a prediction indicating the probability of cancer and need for an operation (e.g. 87%). Using this a surgeon uses their judgment based on the person's age and other complications to take a decision to operate or not. The outcome of the operation is fed back into the system to improve its diagnostic skills and recommendations. In real-time systems such as an autonomous vehicle, there is no time for human involvement in decision making and the machine directly takes the decision, provided that the machine has achieved a desired confidence level.

Internet of Things (IoT) is becoming very popular for automatically managing complex control systems. Its front-end consists of a networked array of sensors providing real-time data from sources needed as inputs for the control system, such as temperature, location, pressure, motion or an image. This data, in its digital form, is fed into an AI based decision-making system, which decides the best action based on the provided input data. IoT systems are used in a variety of applications ranging from optimizing cooling in a data center and enabling self-driving cars to deciding which segment of crops to harvest when

Companies like IBM, Microsoft, Amazon and Google are setting up AI IoT Cloud platforms for their customers, who can bring in data from their sensor networks. Customers develop control algorithms within the IoT Cloud. The IoT platform provides AI and additional algorithm libraries that are needed for control and decision-making. IoT platform providers are also acquiring vast amounts of sensor data to make their platforms even more attractive. They will be able to provision almost any sensor data needed by their customers on a subscription basis. As a result, creating IoT systems will become significantly easier and faster.

Data, in essence, is a digital representation of the reality in the world. As humans, we take our daily decisions based on sensing and analyzing the reality around us with our five senses and using our brain to decide and act upon that data. Internet of Things (IoT) systems work very similarly — with a notable difference. They can decide based on all the thousands of cases they are trained on, 24x7, undistracted, without breaks or the need to sleep.

Drones have become an increasingly useful sourcing tool for IoT data. Drones can capture high-quality images and videos of specific areas at a very low cost. Images and video are excellent sources of data patterns for AI. Describing the content or the subtle uniqueness in images and video clips is often difficult for humans — but not for AI. Machines have become better than humans at pattern recognition and can learn to differentiate subtle patterns in images without human assistance. It is possible to do reliable lip-reading by training AI machines with millions of samples of people talking and the corresponding text. Using image data of vineyards, captured by drones, AI can now predict the best time for harvesting different sections of the vineyard. The color and texture of the grapes provide the patterns for the AI.

As the cost of better decision-making with AI drops steeply, AI will get integrated into almost all products, services, or processes. This will make them a lot smarter and more competitive.

Duality of Intelligence for Decision Making

Human intelligence benefits from an interesting duality of arriving at conclusions. On the one hand arriving at conclusions based on perception of patterns, and on the other reaching conclusions based on logical and rational analysis. Both forms are distinct, but complementary. Machine based intelligence also comes in two forms: AI based decision making based on deep learning which interprets patterns in data to arrive at conclusions, mimicking the perception-based intelligence of our brain, and standard rule-based computing (like in a PC) mimicking the rational intelligence of our brain.

If we were to model the brain based on our general observations it would consist of two parts:

1. Right – Perception based
2. Left – Rational based

Our senses – taste, sight, touch, smell, and hearing – provide patterns to the right part of our brain to generate perceptions. Whereas all our logical interpretations influence the left part and which generates a structured and rational understanding of a situation or a problem.

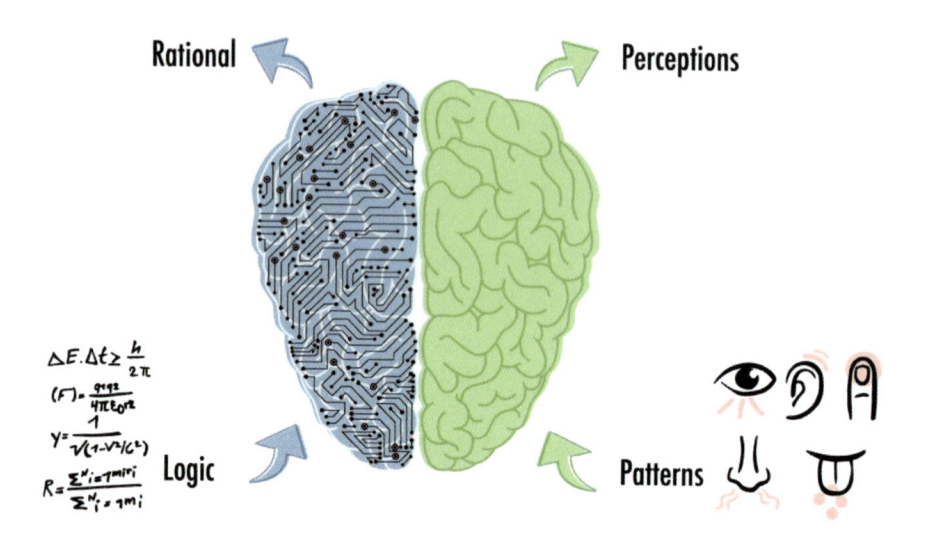

Fig. 4.2 Simplistic model of our brain. Unstructured patterns generate perceptions; structured logic result in rational conclusions

When we study physics or mathematics we are mostly using the rational part of the brain, which is best suited to providing us a logical structure for the subject. However, when we are dealing with patterns created by our senses, we are using the perception part of the brain. Our five senses are the prime sources of patterns for creating perceptions. Since most situations are a mix of logic and patterns, we collaboratively use both rational and perception parts of the brain to arrive at conclusions and make decisions. Both parts, perception and rational, are integral sources of human intelligence.

Both parts of the brain are simultaneously active in all situations. The right part may be busy generating perceptions based on patterns, while simultaneously, for the same situation, the rational part of the brain is busy constructing a rational interpretation of the situation based on some logical structure and comes up with a rational conclusion. Who wins? Right or left-brain? It depends on the situation.

Most AI systems today are based on deep learning, where learning happens through exposing the AI system to tens of thousands of illustrative examples. Deep learning involves absorbing intricate details and subtle nuances in pictures, videos, or sounds into the parameters of the neural network of the AI system. After the training, the AI system is able to perceive the input data based on patterns in images, faces, objects, movements or sounds fed into the system. The AI system's decision-making is based on the perception of the input data patterns, behaving like the right side of the brain – specializing in perceiving patterns.

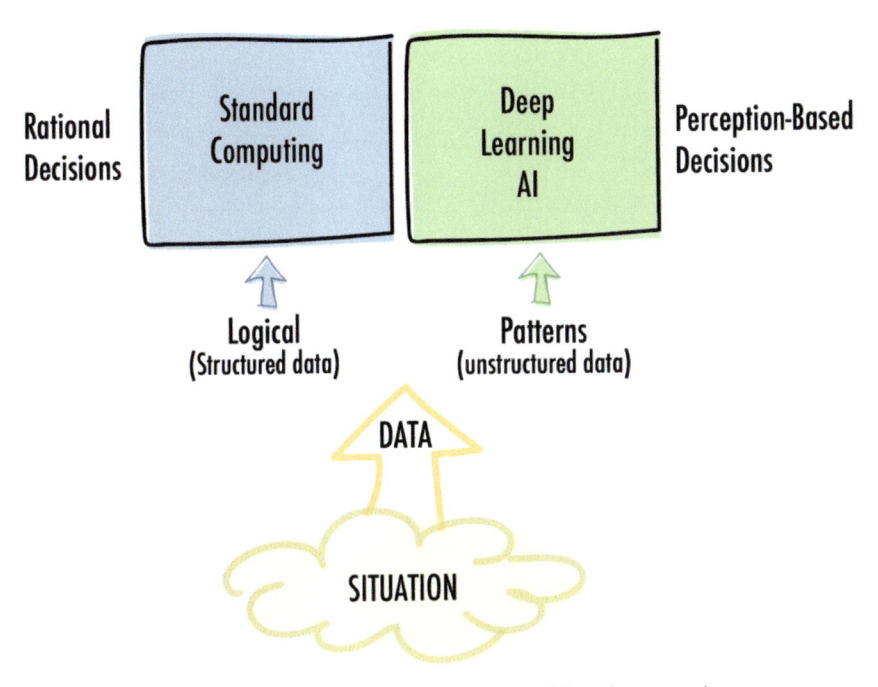

Fig. 4.3 Simplistic model of computing machines for generating perceptions and rational decisions

The left side is about understanding and dealing with logic of the situation. This works more like the standard computing we know from a personal computer (PC) or a smartphone. This is about coding situations that are clearly structured by rules that can be articulated in "IF-THEN-ELSE" logic. It can be compared to the left side of the brain in our simplistic model. Future PCs and Smartphones are very likely to have AI logic integrated. We want to remind our readers that these simplistic models used here are gross approximations of reality. Their purpose is just to illustrate the working of two processes in the brain and to offer a metaphor to illustrate how two forms of computing work in an easy to understand fashion.

We believe that these two forms of computing for decision making — for processing structured (with standard computing) and unstructured data (with deep learning AI) — can be used collaboratively for a much more balanced decision making. Deep learning AI systems are essentially recognition algorithms that automatically convert unstructured pattern based data into structured information that can then be acted upon using standard logic-based computing. This approach helps in addressing the "black box" issues of AI and increases the transparency of decision making. Let us illustrate this with a couple of examples.

- **Surveillance video**: Today most public places are monitored with scores of video cameras. Video data from these can be collectively scrutinized for suspicious activities or people using AI. Once AI concludes based on understanding the video feeds that something suspicious is happening or about to happen it creates an alert with its decision on what is happening together with a recommended action. By doing this AI has translated an unstructured situation based on video sequences into a concrete structured information that something critical has happened or is imminent — eg. a terrorist attack or a terrorist has been identified in a public place. With this structured information, the rational intelligence dealing with structured information can kick in and take a specific decision to act (e.g. vacate the public place). This illustrates how both types of computing can work collaboratively.

- **Traffic management**: Google maps obtains traffic information based on people travelling with smartphones on the road, indicating which segments of roads have normal traffic, slower traffic or traffic jams. Using this information together with other sources of traffic alerts and allows an AI system to predict on how traffic in each segment is likely to evolve over time. Essentially, the AI translates unstructured data of traffic speed data for on various roads into structured information forecasts of how the traffic will be in 15 minutes, in 30 minutes, or in an hour. This forecast information can be used to guide individual drivers via routes that minimize their estimated time of arrival, based on where they are heading.

Both these examples illustrate how AI and standard computing can work hand-in-hand to solve problems in a balanced and collaborative way. AI is essentially used to make sense of the unstructured data patterns and translate it into structured information, which can be transparently and decisively acted upon by standard computing techniques.

This balanced approach can be used to take reliable decisions in complex systems containing mixed sources of unstructured and structured data such as for autonomous vehicles or other robotic solutions. A generic version is illustrated in the following diagram.

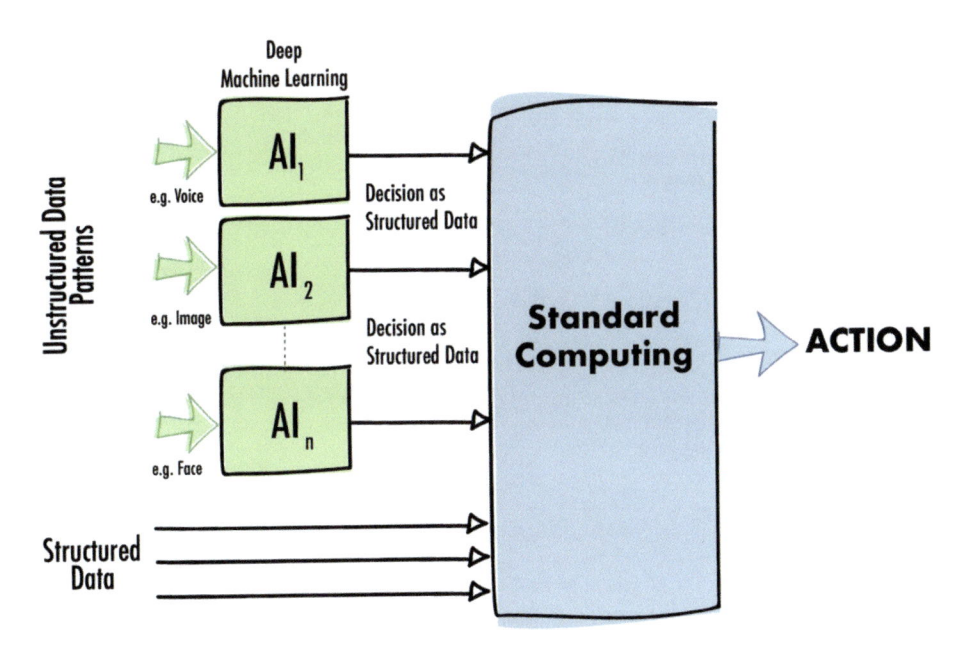

Fig. 4.4 Decision making with a mix of structured and unstructured data. AI converts unstructured data to structured

Use of AI in Business

Just like in the case of the Internet, every business in every industry will benefit, and will very likely be transformed with AI. The following list points out just a few examples of where AI will be applied in various industries. Over time, as the AI technology matures, we believe it will become an integral part of all business processes.

Vertical Industry	Examples
Aerospace	Landing of the rocket boosters — saves millions Autonomous drone taxis Automated landings in extreme weather
Agriculture	Increasing crop yields Harvesting — find optimal timing Minimized watering and pesticides Genetically modified food research
Construction	Safety — fire, crowd management Optimize building criteria Discovery of errors in plans Smart home automation
Defence	Drone warfare Breaking enemy codes Best strategy for attack Abnormal activity detection Cyberwarfare
Education	Adapting learning program to your level — personalization Understanding a person's level of proficiency Virtual mentors

Energy	Smart grid — predicting the needs of when and where
	Simulation of future energy needs
	Home energy management
	Disaster recovery management
Entertainment	Games
	Personalized entertainment
	AI generated music, art ..
	Voice assisted entertainment
Financial Services / Insurance	Insurance claims
	Loan approvals
	Investment consulting
	Forex trading
Food & Beverage	Personalized diet management
	Reducing waste in food production, storage, and delivery
Government	Security
	Tax
	Elections
	Chatbots
Healthcare	Diagnosis
	Prevention
	Telemedicine — AI doctor
	Mining medical records
	Designing treatment plans
	Precision medicine
	Drug creation
Manufacturing	Robotics
	IoT
	Smart Factory

	Logistics
	Quality control
	Preventive maintenance
Retail	Online retail — consumer insights, recommendations, product selector
	Inventory management, article placement
	Advertising
	Customer service
	Customer understanding — real needs, concerns
	Demand forecasting
	Product search ranking
	Product and deals recommendations
	Merchandising placements
	Fraud detection
	Translations
Tourism	Tour guides — personalized
	Customer service
	AI powered travel consultants
	Predictive booking management
Transportation	Route optimization — people and goods
	Autonomous driving, people, and goods
	Reducing human errors
	Traffic control
Personal	Personal assistant — Chatbots
	Personal health trainer
	Home management

Fig. 4.5 Use of AI in business - by vertical industry

Similarly, AI will become an integral part in almost all horizontal business functions. Here are a few examples.

Horizontal Business Function	Examples
Customer Service	AI driven customer service and problem-solving Understanding of customer real needs and concerns Understanding problem areas
Finance	Risk management Vendor and customer assessment Controlling Expense management Reporting
Human Resources	Hiring Human assessment Training Motivation management
IT	Predictive maintenance Security Spam management
Legal	Legal risk assessment Best legal approach recommendation Due diligence verification
Logistics	Optimize and monitor logistics Preventive disruption management Problem spotting and solving

Procurement	Supplier assessment and reliability
	Supplier research
	Tender management
Production	Robotics
	Assembly line monitoring and optimization
	Logistics
	Quality control
Sales & Marketing	Automated personalized advertising
	All aspects of CRM
	Customer understanding and insights
	Marketing automation — messages, personalize
	Analytics
	Next best offer
	Automated proposals
	Sales consultants

Fig. 4.6 Use of AI — by horizontal business functions

5. The Role of AI in Technology

Technology has had a profound impact on our lives. It has to allowed us to create astonishing tools and machines that make our lives easier and more secure, like cranes, the automobile or x-ray scanners. We have significantly reduced famine, plague and war, doubled our life expectancy, and live a much more comfortable life compared with just a couple of hundred years ago. Most of this can be attributed to technological advancements. Our intelligence together with our ability to create powerful tools has moved us to the top of the food chain. The invention of artificial intelligence, combined with other modern technologies, like Internet of Things, Big Data, and robots will now take us to new productivity levels, far beyond today's possibilities.

The impact of artificial intelligence on technology, in general, is huge. It adds learning capability to machines and improves the decisions that machines need to make. This is done through software and neural networks, which have improved based on the huge data transfer capacities of recent computing generation, and the highly parallel computing capabilities of modern chips with specialized parallel processing architectures. All computers, machines, and robots are directed by software. The programs that run them define their performance and capabilities. The logic of software is based on input, some operations and calculations being done on the input producing an output.

Since artificial intelligence enables the machine to learn from this flow, from input to output, by being trained or by observing the results, the software can adapt itself to perform better in the future. Today this is often done through neural networks, whose multi-level pattern-recognitions create self-improving algorithms based on observing enormous data streams. These algorithms can yield better results than algorithms created by human developers in traditional ways, giving artificial intelligence an edge over human-created ones, especially in cases where there are many complex parameters, and large volumes of data over time. Better algorithms enable better software that even improves over time. This brings cognitive capabilities to other technologies running on software, and because most technologies run on software, the impact is huge.

Computer chips, sensors, the Internet, cloud computing, apps, robots, drones and augmented reality are some examples where artificial intelligence based software improves the performance. But also for more complex systems like enterprise resource systems, mobile phones, and large-scale traffic control systems, artificial intelligence advances the capabilities, performance, and quality of software and machines significantly. It also adds new capabilities like voice and image recognition that enable new functions and more efficient and convenient user interfaces. The capability of machines to learn also allows more complex use cases, where several steps are needed to perform a given task.

Initial technological areas where artificial intelligence has the most profound impact are Big Data, Internet of things and robotics. The increasing digitalization of many areas of our lives and businesses have created enormous data pools and constant data streams. The area of Big Data focuses on datasets that are so large or complex that traditional data processing application software is inadequate to deal with them. Big Data is often generated by combing application specific data with external data sources, thus making the data sets very complex and difficult to handle.

A simple example is using an app to go to a restaurant. Your smartphone knows the time of the day, your current location, as well as your destination. An algorithm can calculate the best route to get from A to B. This information can be combined with weather information,

information about road traffic, public transportation options, taxi and Uber-like options or local bike sharing options as well as the availability of bike paths on the way. Predictive data can simulate how the situation is likely to change in the near and distant future. The complexity of handling such a digital service becomes enormous. Artificial Intelligence can make better sense of the data, identify patterns and learn from your behavior and the result. How much time did it actually take to reach the destination and how is it different from what was projected? What factors caused delays? An intelligent routing system based on artificial intelligence can produce significantly better results than simple routing algorithms. And it can improve over time as it learns what factors matter and what personal behaviors impact the result.

Other examples are understanding medical images, optimizing plant fertilization and watering, simulating climate change predictions and financial transactions. In companies, customer behavior, digital marketing and advertising and human resource performance are other examples of Big Data applications where artificial intelligence can play a big role.

More and more data sets are produced by real world sensors that have emerged through the growth of Internet of Things (IoT), where smart and connected little machines perform simple tasks in all parts of our lives. Scales, cameras, coffee machines, thermostats, gates, video surveillance systems are only a few such examples. IoT is characterized by internetworking of physical devices. Often it contains sensors to generate data, an ability to communicate this data through the Internet and then acting on this data. A surveillance camera generates a series of pictures, uploads them to the cloud, where image processing software detects the alarming situation and informs the user via an app, while the camera sounds a built in alarm. Then based on the movement of objects, the camera can follow moving objects or can be controlled via an app from anywhere in the world. Both the application of IoT devices and the sheer amount of data they produce are creating a lot of use cases that benefit from artificial intelligence. Most of the recent devices are labeled smart or intelligent, like Nuki's door knob that automatically opens your door as you approach with your smartphone, but just like the personal voice assistants, the intelligence can still be questioned. Financial services company IHS forecasts that the

IoT market will grow from an installed base of 15.4 billion devices in 2015 to 30.7 billion devices in 2020 and 75.4 billion in 2025, so IoT becomes a big driver and beneficiary of artificial intelligence capabilities.

Another area where artificial intelligence is being deployed on a big scale is robots. The field of robotics, an interdisciplinary branch of engineering and science that includes mechanical engineering, electrical engineering, computer science, materials and others, has embraced artificial intelligence to give robots cognitive capabilities, going from simple pre-programmed capabilities to more complex, context-aware applications of high quality. Robots combine a lot of technological capabilities and also incorporate technologies like Big Data or IoT. Robots come in many shapes or forms like manufacturing machines, self-driving cars, and drones. These cognitive capabilities allow new use cases like monitoring crop health by drones, resulting in better fertilization and use of pesticides. The cost saving and quality improvements in comparison to traditional models, like human inspection or airplane monitoring, are huge. According to a study by Informa Economics, corn, soybean and wheat farmers could save an estimated $1.3 billion annually by using drones to increase crop yields and reduce input costs.

Robots are also an area of great dispute and cause of human anxiety. In the industrial revolution, people feared that automated machines would take away a lot of their jobs, and science fiction movies have often portrayed robots as stronger than humans, once they turn to their own self-created motives. If these motives are bad, the impact on humanity is existential. We should be aware that humans create the technology and give robots their tasks.

The new and evolving capability of artificial intelligence, and its impact on other technologies, has added a lot of complexity to an already difficult-to-understand and difficult-to-master landscape of technologies. The complexity of creating the best solution for a given use case and the impact for businesses if they get it wrong are limiting factors for take-up of the technologies in many areas. Fortunately, an ecosystem of software, tools, and services is being created at a fast pace, fueled by corporate and venture investments in the promising new area of artificial intelligence. One can find ready-to-use and proven solution in all areas of technology. If you are looking for complex industry solutions, if you are looking to optimize your enterprise processes, are looking for capabilities, tools and components like image recognition, voice understanding and translations, neural networks or core technologies like neural networks, there is a growing ecosystem of artificial intelligence-enhanced solutions and services that you can tap into.

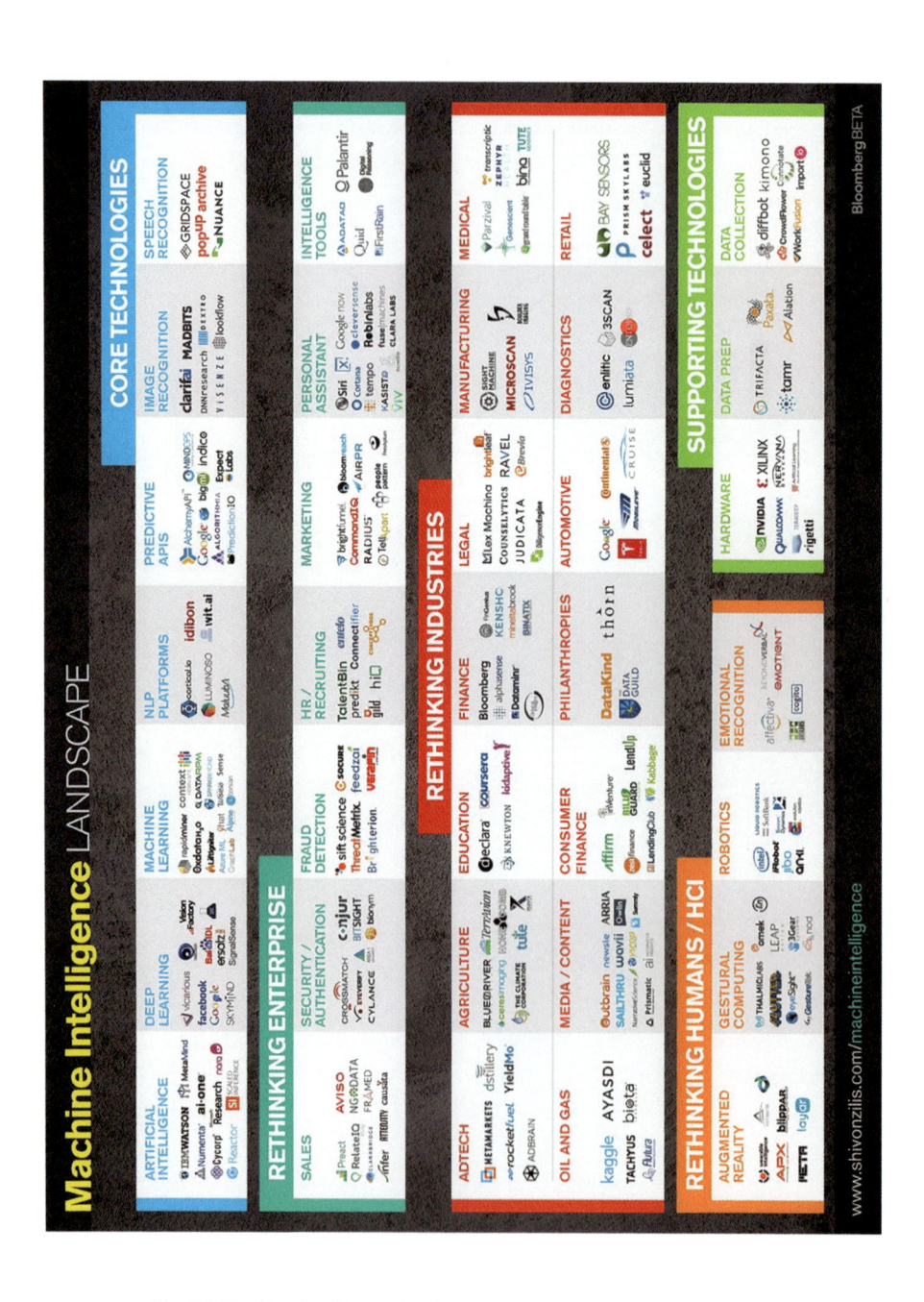

Fig. 5.1 Machine intelligence landscape — Shivon Zilis, BloombergBETA

AI&U – Translating Artificial Intelligence into Business

Another ecosystem visualization focuses on core areas of enterprises:

Fig. 5.2 TOPBOTs overview of AI companies and services.

Businesses now need to figure out how to create value for their customers using artificial intelligence and what business model makes it competitive and profitable.

6. The Role of AI in Business

Can you think of an industry that does not benefit from intelligence? We believe that AI can enhance all business areas and will fundamentally impact most industries and businesses. The reason is very simple — artificial intelligence allows you to make better decisions for both simple and very complex tasks. It does so by understanding and evaluating all the parameters and factors that influence it. It can leverage complete sets of data, it can better understand the influencing factors and produce an answer that is more reliable than humans alone can. We are seeing the evolution of new AI-based tools and services, that can help run better organizations, optimize the core business processes as well as create better products and services for customers. Continuous technological advancement in computing power, connectivity, neural networks will fuel the development of more and better AI, which can be leveraged in business.

Businesses are constantly evolving organizational entities, striving to create and deliver the best goods and services to consumers. They do so in an ever changing world, often in a highly competitive environment. Customer needs change, new competitors enter the market, laws and regulations change, communication channels change, technology evolves providing new capabilities. AI is the one new capability that has far-reaching implications on many aspects of the business and industries they operate in. It is a new lubricant of all business operations by enabling better decisions on all levels.

Some examples where artificial intelligence can help businesses in making better decisions are:

- Should you hire this person?
- Who is your best customer?

- What services need to be improved?
- What features do your customers love?
- What products will go out of demand soon?
- Which are suppliers with declining quality and reliability?
- How to train your employees better?
- What is the risk of a contract?
- What is the best business model option?

Based on the learning effects, each new decision can be used to better train the system by observing the results of the decision. Artificial intelligence can be used to create more intelligent products. A smartphone that knows where you want to go next and organizes the way. A voice assistant which can book a restaurant table dinner this evening, informing and coordinating the participants. A refrigerator that replenishes itself and helps with a healthy diet on a daily basis. A self-driving car. A security drone. A CRM system that automatically focuses on helping you develop your best customers. A HR tool that helps you hire the most suitable person. A corporate communication tool that ensure transparency and assesses the motivation level of your employees. These are just a few examples of intelligent products that are likely to evolve from artificial intelligence capabilities.

7. Part 1 — Concluding Remarks

Can machines be intelligent? Can machines learn? What can we do with intelligent machines? These are questions that have intrigued us for several decades. With AI becoming integrated into real applications during the last few years, quite a few answers are emerging. We have seen that the machines can learn in a manner quite comparable to humans. They can be labeled intelligent, i.e exhibiting cognitive capabilities of learning, decision making and problem-solving. AI with ML neural networks is at an early stage of development, addressing relatively narrow and very specific tasks. AI has been proven very capable in pattern recognition tasks, where the machine learns to accurately interpret patterns in images, video, sound etc. They make reliable decisions in areas like speech, object, and face recognition, language translations, medical diagnosis, scene descriptions and language understanding. The unique value of AI comes from automatically making better, faster and accurate decisions in areas which are not clearly defined by precise rules. All aspects of any business benefit from better decisions made faster, automatically, and inexpensively.

We have scratched only the surface of intelligence in this book. Intelligence — as experienced in humans — goes beyond decision making and problem-solving. Areas like creativity, insights, imagination, judgment, relationships, conscience and emotional intelligence are in a different domain. The connection between emotions and rational elements in decision making is quite complex and not yet understood. The intelligence of our brain has many more dimensions, and is far more potent than AI exhibited by machines today. It is interesting to speculate what could happen when we network thousands or millions of AI neural networks together, operating like one entity. Is that how our brain is structured, with different areas of the brain responsible for specialized tasks like speech, vision etc.? Another area pursued by researchers, including Elon Musk, CEO of Tesla, is interconnecting our brain with AI thus extending the capacity of our brain to seamlessly tap into AI for specific expertise in new languages or skills. Imagine being able to tap into the entire Google database directly and seamlessly from your brain — as if all that knowledge were to reside in your brain.

In the second part of the book, we will use the newly gained insight into artificial intelligence and apply it to how to leverage it for your business.

Part 2 – Leveraging AI for Your Business

Introduction Part 2

Welcome to the second part of the book. Let us warn you: AI is likely to come faster than you might think, and the impact on your business may be far greater than you can imagine today. In fact, as you are reading this, AI is already creeping into your business systems and software. And while you might be wondering how this can happen, several new AI start-ups are launching and fast competitors are disrupting your business. It is not the big robots, though they will also come, but it is in all the small stealth changes, making processes and tools more effective, adding new capabilities to businesses, that will threaten your business. In fact, as we are writing this, AI is going into every piece of software, making it better and faster and cheaper. This has happened in the consumer space with Virtual Assistants such as Apple Siri, Google Maps, Apple Photos, Facebook, which are now part of your everyday life. Software is eating the world and AI is eating software. And now industries will be disrupted. Welcome to a new world, where Artificial Intelligence is not only real and here to stay, but where leveraging AI will be a critical competitive factor for surviving in the future. Let us take you on a journey, and present a number of tools than can help you and your business survive and thrive in the age of Artificial Intelligence.

8. Why Now? AI — The Critical Ingredient

"Artificial Intelligence is an amazing renaissance to technology, business and society. Machine Learning is a horizontal enabling layer. It will empower and improve every business, every government organization, every philanthropy ... basically, there is not an institution in the world that cannot be improved with Machine Learning."

- **Jeff Bezos, CEO and Founder, Amazon. May 2017, www.internetassociation.org**

"In an 'AI first' world we are rethinking all our products and applying Machine Learning and AI to solve user problems. We are doing that across every one of our products."

- **Sundar Pichai, CEO Google, I/O 2017 Keynote**

"Anytime you see a pattern …. AI is very good for a needle in a haystack problems and changes in patterns."

- **Eric Schmidt, Executive President Alphabet (Google), RSA Conference, 2017**

"AI is the next platform. All future applications, all future capabilities for all companies will be built on AI."

- **Marc Benioff, CEO Salesforce.com**

"I think we're in the phase where AI will change pretty much every major industry."

- **Andrew Ng, renowned machine learning expert and chief scientist at Baidu**

"Artificial intelligence is the 'ultimate breakthrough.' If I broadly talk about AI including machine learning, the thing that's been most exciting in the last five years is this one specialized branch of 'deep neural network' that is fundamentally giving us human perception, whether it is speech or image recognition, and that's just magical to see."

- **Satya Nadella, CEO Microsoft**

"In the next 10 to 20 years, AI is going to be "extremely helpful" in managing our lives….The risk of artificial intelligence software becoming super smart is way out in the future"

- **Bill Gates, Philanthropist, Founder Microsoft**

"I feel this is a profoundly hopeful time….Cognitive healthcare is real and here and can change almost everything about healthcare….Cognition means that precision medicine is coming alive….Digital is foundation to everything. But competitive advantage will come from cognitive. And there is a land rush on AI at the moment."

- **Ginni Rometty, CEO IBM, HIMSS 2017 conference in Orlando**

"I see an AI first world….I think very strongly that intelligent applications will fundamentally change the way you do work in the enterprise and the way you collaborate with your trading partners outside of the enterprise….We need the system to tell us what to do. Based on algorithms of that data and inputs that are in that data bank."

- **Bill McDermott, CEO SAP**

"In 30 years, a robot will likely be on the cover of Time Magazine as the best CEO. Machines will do what human beings are incapable of doing. Machines will partner and cooperate with humans, rather than become mankind's biggest enemy."

- **Jack Ma, CEO Alibaba**

"The [AI] companion in the Vision Next 100 car is just that: a real companion that gets to know you as a person and responds to you as an individual, I firmly believe this is not a threat to us, it's much more a huge opportunity to all of us — mobility become more versatile. It will be effortless, available on demand and tailor-made for all our customers' individual needs."

- **Harald Krueger, CEO BMW**

"Artificial intelligence is the key to the digital future of the Volkswagen Group"

- **Martin Hofmann, CIO Volkswagen**

"Success in creating AI could be the biggest event in the history of our civilization."

- **Stephen Hawking, Astrophysicist, Futurist, Guardian, May 15, 2017**

CEOs of many leading companies are already betting their companies future on AI. They have taken the "AI-First" approach to products, services and internal processes. They recognize that AI has the potential to improve all aspects of a business — product development, manufacturing, management, hiring, training, finance, marketing, sales, and service. Just as the internet disrupted every existing business model and forced a reordering of industry, artificial intelligence will require us to imagine how computing works all over again. Many benefits such as ease of use, higher accuracy, better speed, deeper personalization or cost reduction result from background improvements through AI in the quality of product, service and processes. That is why many companies are talking about baking in AI capabilities into all their products, services and processes. AI is perceived as a wonder ingredient that makes even a product we used yesterday like Siri, Translate or Maps better, easier or cheaper.

Many AI projects can be split into two stages:

1. **AI for Real World Recognition**: The first stage is to apply AI for interfacing machines with the real world. The real world is analog and unstructured, consisting of faces, voice, body language, images, scenes, weather etc. Advances in machine learning have enabled recognition of speech, gestures, faces, objects, and patterns converting the real world data into accurate and useful digital information. This step converts unstructured analog information of the real world to structured and categorized information needed for your business to leverage.

2. **AI for Business Model Innovation:** The second stage for AI is to leverage this new structured information for your business model for innovation; this is where new value is generated by your business. This step is at the core of your real differentiation and competitiveness. The challenge for most businesses resides in the success of stage 2.

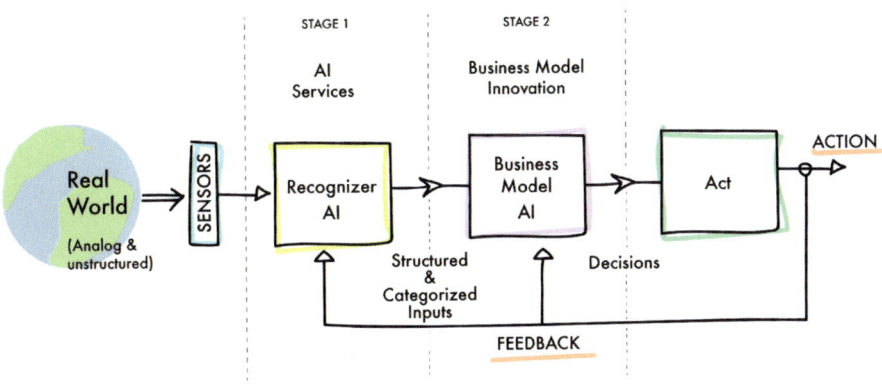

Fig. 8.1 Two stages of AI projects - Understanding the real world and business innovation

We will use self-driving cars as an example to illustrate this process. Stage 1 is all about understanding the environment of the car. Firstly, AI is used to recognize and interpret accurately the environment of the car with sensors such as LIDARs, radar, cameras, motor data, speech data of passengers, weather and traffic information etc. Stage 2 is to make sense of all this information and leverage it to carry out the right actions that make autonomous driving feasible. It is how this is done that will differentiate a Tesla from BMW or Mercedes. The decisions made in stage 2 will determine if passengers and lawmakers are satisfied with the quality, safety and comfort of the ride in all possible situations. Stage 1 in the process is becoming easier for businesses thanks to the intensity of ongoing AI research, startup efforts, and business endeavors of some key players. Recognition algorithms are more readily available via open source, AI platforms, and AI startups developing algorithms to interface the real world to machines.

Let us consider some examples of early success with AI. In "The Promise of Artificial Intelligence" (https://vimeo.com/215926017) Frank Chen of Andressen Horowitz has categorized various areas of AI that have made very good progress. These examples provide several useful ideas, both for stage 1 and stage 2, in the process of developing AI solutions for your business. He states that AI will be integrated into every important piece of software and applications. In today's world software runs every product, service, and even entire businesses.

Chen says, in every major technology upheaval, a key technology component becomes significantly cheaper and its inclusion in many aspects of businesses and lifestyle creates a revolution. With the Industrial Revolution the steam engine, internal combustion engine, electricity and motors have made machine driven "muscle power" cheaper and easily available. In the last 50 years use of data has become cheaper through digitalization, computing and communication. AI is next. It will make prediction and data-based decision making much cheaper and better than alternatives, making it a de facto ingredient in all applications. Chen uses relevant examples to show six areas where AI has already shown amazing promise for significant change. Here is a summary:

1. Self-driving vehicles
2. Understanding the world
3. Creating content
4. Predicting future
5. Optimizing complex systems
6. Language understanding

1. **Self-Driving Vehicles** — planes, trains, trucks, buses, ships, cars, carts etc.
   - It will seem odd to our grandchildren that something cannot get from A to B all by itself.
   - Things will come to you on their own.
   - Drones can follow and assist you in activities.
   - Drones can save lives in dangerous situations or finding survivors in disaster areas.
   - Self-driving vehicles or drones can deliver blood in emergencies.

2. **Understanding the World**
   - Computer vision for "seeing" and image recognition.
   - Tests consistently show that AI has over 95% accuracy, better than best humans in certain areas, and only when trained on those areas.
   - Spotting individual objects within images.
   - Ability to identify objects with specific color and characteristics.

- Precision farming: identifying plants in a field that need fertilizers and avoid spraying the entire field with fertilizer or pesticide.
- Automatic checkout in stores — all items in shopping cart are recognized and listed.
- Robot in a hardware store visually recognizing what you need and showing you where to find it in the store.
- Ability to recognize content in a sequence of pictures and automatically creating a narrative of how they are linked.

3. **Creating Content** — articles, tweets, stories, music, art and application software.
   - Generate detailed step-by-step recipes from a series of pictures or a video.
   - Generate photorealistic images from a description or a sketch.
   - Generate music based on parameters provided.
   - Creation of trailer for movies — using IBM Watson — a big help to editors even if it needs human tuning of the final trailer.
   - Generate application software using existing code modules.

4. **Predicting future events**
   - Decide which videos to translate or dub from another language by predicting the success of a video or movie based on the success pattern of videos in a specific country.
   - Predict a person's identity automatically from the way the person moves or handles the smartphone.
   - Predict how you will be received based on the physical behavior of the individual you want to interact with.
   - Predict heart-related problems based on the data generated from the Apple Watch.

5. **Optimizing Complex Systems**
   - Optimize driving routes for people based on their driving style, other people on the road, and current congestion situation.
   - Optimizing the configuration of soccer player placements in accordance with each player's strengths and that of the

- opposing team in a match for a given strategy.
- Software optimization that result in much denser code and faster execution times. 60% speed improvements are possible.
- Getting better than average results on the stock market.
- Energy consumption in large organizations. Google achieved 20-15% savings on energy consumption in their data center by allowing AI to control their energy systems — monitoring 120 parameters from which servers are running at what load to cooling needs etc.
- Optimizing the path/route taken to navigate large store aisles according to a given shopping list thus minimizing grocery shopping time.

6. **Language understanding**
   - Speech recognition — we can communicate information 3x faster by speech vs. written.
   - Understanding the context of what is written. Google Smart-Reply can automatically formulate answers to emails.
   - Understanding and collating content derived from multiple reports on a specific topic and generating one synopsis that integrates critical elements from each text.
   - Textio can understand a job description and suggest changes with right words and language, in order to appeal to the person who is most appropriate for the job.
   - Everlaw looks through all the documents in a legal trial process during the e-discovery phase to categorize them and show lawyers which documents are relevant for any specific topic in the case, to ensure that the lawyers do not miss something out

These are some current examples where AI is making a significant change in business processes. The list is growing by the day. You should take these as samples and inspiration providing new ideas for your business. AI provides a myriad of opportunity to reinvent your business just as was possible with the emergence of new technologies such as computing, the internet and mobile devices. Business model innovation — the stage 2 in this process — is where most focus needs to be devoted as this is what will truly allow for differentiation from competition and prompt a unique core strength for your organization. Next, we will illustrate using a few case studies and show how some businesses are innovating with AI.

9. AI Case Studies

Tesla: Autonomous Driving using Artificial Intelligence

"Full autonomy is going to come a hell of a lot faster than anyone thinks it will and I think what we've got under development is going to blow people's minds," said Elon Musk, CEO of Tesla, in a press release press release in August 2016.

Fig. 9.1 Tesla, prime example of sensor based autonomous driving with AI

Did you know Tesla has never turned an annual profit and is not predicted to do so until 2020. So how does this firm have a market value on par with some of the world's largest automobile manufacturers? Tesla is not just an automaker, but also a technology and design company with a focus on energy innovation. By using the latest computing technologies to bring new benefits to its customers, like autonomous driving and related services, it has disrupted the market.

Autonomous cars are vehicles capable of sensing the environment surrounding and navigating without human input. To achieve this, Tesla first used cameras and radars to detect and understand obstacles on the road to help steer its autonomous vehicles. The problem that emerged however is that sometimes these sensors could be tricked by complex and seemingly illogical situations. For example, a low bridge with a dip underneath it may appear to be a solid roadblock from far away (this also happens to the human perception, by the way). In response to this, Tesla began collecting data from other Tesla vehicles to observe how human drivers behaved at a particular location. If other vehicles did not brake consistently, then no braking would be required for autonomous driving. Similarly, when the observing AI noticed drivers slowing at certain locations, the AI implemented mild breaking for autonomous vehicles. These decisions are combined to data from sensors to formulate the best decision for any given situation. In doing so, Tesla built a map based on artificial intelligence, and is employing it as an input for all its cars in combination with the radar. It even works in very difficult visibility situations, providing additional safety for drivers and their cars.

For all of this Tesla is using artificial intelligence algorithms which also define the confidence levels. This means if there is a 99.99 percent confidence level that there is an obstruction, it will add a full break for that designated location on the map and combine that with the sensor input, at any given time.

Tesla estimates that, after 10 billion kilometers are recorded/combined from Tesla cars, their car will be 10 times safer than regular human driven cars. By driving this distance it helps the AI to learn and find the best decision for any given moment. The advantage of this self-learning method is that it can resolve some of the most complicated situations for the sensors of cameras and radars. The more drivers will use it, the smarter it will become. This combination of learning from observing behavior (of drivers) from a wide range of drivers and combining it with input from sensors of the local car illustrates the power of AI for autonomous vehicles. It can overcome complex hurdles in discovering and reacting to obstacles on the road based on sensory data streams in combination with behavioral pattern. There are many similar approaches taken in Internet of Things solutions worldwide.

Some key insights from this example:

CEO is driving it — Elon Musk is the driving force behind Tesla's advancement in Artificial Intelligence. With his wiz kid science background, passion and engagements in leading AI initiatives like OPEN AI, Musk makes AI the center of his work. This makes it clear for the organization that AI is not just a nice to have technology but a key building block of the future of the company. Elon Musk makes it a top priority and makes sure all understand.

It's a way to outcompete other players — By leveraging AI, Tesla is able to achieve new levels of safety compared to today's human driven vehicles. While many competitors are playing catch-up by adding sensors to their vehicles to allow them to support drivers in certain situations, Tesla is fully committed to letting AI deliver self-learning autonomous driving.

It provides true value — Next to improved safety, Tesla's AI-based autonomous driving offers a new level of comfort and frees-up personal time for its customers and, in doing so, creates a new value proposition. In addition, autonomous vehicles create even more value for customers by exercising the capacity to perform other services while not being in use.

Its value improves over time — Tesla vehicles are known to improve over time, just as smartphones improve with new app capabilities, Tesla vehicles are updated continuously. AI means their capabilities keep on improving, thus making them more valuable.

Salesforce

"We cannot solve our problems with the same kind of thinking that we used when we created them," Albert Einstein.

Fig. 9.2 Einstein from Salesforce applies AI to customer data

With this statement in mind Salesforce set out to rework its popular suite of customer facing cloud-based business products for companies, based on AI called Einstein. After a long planning period and the strategic investments in AI talent and companies, the AI enhanced suite was released in early 2017. You, as a business person, might know the challenges with CRM systems and other customer facing tools in service and marketing. Today's tools give you a means to manage your data but the true value of this information lies between the lines and has to be extracted from the figures. You have to build models to understand the data and act upon it in such a way that you can leverage its full potential. Most implementations we have seen in our careers do not even come close to utilizing the potential. People get bogged down in transferring the data into the system, keeping it up to date and relevant and doing mass actions to act on it. But, since AI is good at understanding data, and detecting trends, associations and causes, it can prepare the right decisions and allow you to act or even takes control of acting with the right response at the right moment. Some new areas are discovering new insights about your customers like who are your best customers, predicting outcomes to make smarter decisions like what offer to send to customers and identifying which customers are considering leaving you. It recommends the next sales, service, and marketing actions.

By integrating AI in its suite of cloud-based applications, Einstein is removing the complexity of AI and enabling any company to deliver smarter, personalized and more predictive customer experiences. For example the Salesforce CRM Software delivers automated customer insights to its user based on AI. Powered by advanced machine learning, deep learning, predictive analytics, natural language processing and smart data discovery, Salesforce claims that Einstein's models will be automatically customized for every single customer. It will learn, self-tune, and get smarter with every interaction and additional piece of data. And this intelligence is embedded directly into the context of your business data.

Salesforce's cloud-first strategy and experience and understanding of ecosystems plays nicely in leveraging AI on a bigger scale. The Einstein API allows 3rd party developers to create their own apps, utilizing the API resources and integrating with customer data. One example of integrating AI-based vision with AI-based customer preference can be taken from real estate app "The Dreamhouse". Customers are shown real estate images, compiled by Einstein's AI from a pool of offerings, based on their profiles behavior preferences built by the CRM AI. Sound impressive? It even improves over time. If Einstein is anywhere near as useful as Salesforce claims, the technology will supplant some human workers — maybe a lot of them.

Some key insights from this example:

Leverage the value of data — and CRM systems are likely to have lots of data. Instead of people wasting time trying to make sense of it and acting upon it, let AI do the work. It will be a lot faster and more thorough.

Learns and improves over time — customer data grows over time, in fact most of the insights come during the customer life cycle. AI continues to learn and improve its learning to better suit your customers preferences.

Improve all aspects — once you have mastered the AI technology it allows you to improve all aspects of your offering. Salesforce has integrated Einstein AI into all of its cloud offerings thus improving the way it works and adding new AI-based capabilities.

Build a platform — Einstein AI enhances the Salesforce offering, making it more valuable to its customers and allowing Salesforce to charge a premium price. By integrating additional data sources and providing an API to external sources it increases its value exponentially, while the competition is struggling and falling behind.

Leverage 3rd party developers — One company cannot create all value scenarios and apps for such diverse industries. By providing access to Einstein Services like image recognition and coupling those with Salesforce-based data services, Salesforce customers get a richer set of software services without requiring development by its customers.

H&R BLOCK

I have yet to meet a person who enjoys filing income tax returns every year. 140m US citizens file tax returns every year. Most need professional help from tax consultants. H&R BLOCK is one of the largest tax consultants in the USA with over 10,000 offices filing tax returns for 11 million Americans. They employ 70,000 tax experts for preparing tax returns. H&R BLOCK has been losing business in the last few years to online tax programs like TurboTax, hence were seeking a strategy that would craft a more engaging, interactive and rewarding experience for clients. HR Block CEO Bill Cobb's goal was to "reinvent the retail experience of taxpayers." The solution? Use Artificial Intelligence as a tax specialist to accompany and assist the HR Block representative in the process of preparing tax returns together with their clients.

H&R Block opted for IBM Watson as their preferred AI platform. To train the Watson AI system as a tax specialist: it was fed with the enormous 74,000 pages of Federal tax code and thousands of pages of tax law changes every year. This is a vast amount of information to take in, sort through, and decide how it applies to each customer's tax situation, depending on issues such as marital status, job losses, dependents, mortgages, and capital gains, but Watson does this with ease. "This speaks to Watson's strengths as a learning machine," said Rob Enderle, an analyst with the Enderle Group. "Unless you are an incredibly unusual person, there is no way you can know how to optimize a tax payment or return absolutely. There is simply too much information to learn and so much new [data] being created that even if you were able to read and understand it all, by the time you were done you'd still be terribly out of date." Since Watson can collect and categorize data, it can absorb new tax information in real time, keeping it up to date with new laws and adjustments to old laws, Enderle said. In addition, the best tax experts at H&R Block, train Watson on the proper response to thousands of customer questions that have cropped up in the past years. As a result, Watson becomes a central repository of tax laws, top expert knowledge, and the history of all questions and responses. This knowledge and expertise becomes instantly accessible to all tax consultants of H&R Block. "Once [Watson is] fully trained, H&R Block should be able to show absolute proof that their customers pay less taxes because the system will be able to generate reports that accurately showcase this result in aggregate," Enderle added.

(http://www.computerworld.com/article/3173283/artificial-intelligence/hr-block-turns-to-ai-to-tackle-your-tax-return.html)

When a client sits down with an H&R Block tax preparer, the preparer asks questions that are also provided to Watson. This information involves tax-relevant events that happened to the customer during the previous tax year – home purchases, marriage, birth of a child, a child entering school or a family member leaving the military. Watson uses that information to draw insights into the tax implications of those new jobs, home sales, and marriages and offers recommendations. During the session, the customer follows along on a monitor as his or her taxes are prepared, and Watson suggests different possibilities. All decisions are taken by humans — the tax preparer and the taxpayer — but guided by the expertise and accuracy of Watson AI. Most customers find the process not just very interesting, but at the same time rewarding since they generally receive higher refunds resulting from lower tax liabilities because of Watson AI's thoroughness and accuracy. Human tax consultants are able to secure refunds for only about 75% people who file taxes. H&R Block with Watson AI promises refunds for up to 85% of customers. Customer return rate is another benchmark for H&R Block. They aim to raise the return rate from 75% to 80%.

Some key insights from this example:

Expert knowledge aggregation — Learning, classification, referencing and storage of massive amounts of data is a unique ability of Watson AI systems. Stored data can be continuously and immediately updated. This allows AI systems to draw from a vast range of up-to-date knowledge for each case. The system is ever evolving and learns and updates itself with every new case.

AI recommends and human Decides — We humans are not yet used to taking advice from machines in critical personal areas such as taxes, health and law. Advice from humans is more comforting and trustworthy, even if humans are not as knowledgeable as machines. We feel better hearing about a diagnosis from a human doctor than from a machine, even if the doctor made the diagnosis based on the results from a machine. Watson doesn't cut out humans completely. It aids the process and lets humans do their job better.

AI platform — a fast-track to results — AI platforms provide a shortcut to benefiting from AI technology. Amazon, IBM, Google, and Microsoft offer AI platforms for quick development of solutions, without the need to hire many AI technology specialists. H&R Block remains focused on its core business of tax consulting and just simply leverages the IBM Watson platform for AI. This gave them the first-mover advantage in offering the benefits of AI to tax-paying customers seeking better service and rewards.

Big Data is heaven for AI, hell for humans — As discussed in the first part of this book, too much data overwhelms us and leaves us disoriented and confused resulting in decision paralysis or just plain poor decisions. In contrast, AI relishes data. Its decision making quality and accuracy improves with additional data. Massive tax codes and constant updates are handled by AI with ease.

10. Discovering Your AI Opportunity

So, are you inspired to go on an exciting journey with your company? Do you have ideas in mind where Artificial Intelligence can help your business? Now is the time to start working on the opportunity for your organization with Artificial Intelligence. It is a time to think beyond existing conventions, put some of your bias and fears aside and be open to experience a world of new possibilities. We have conducted numerous workshops on finding opportunities for Artificial Intelligence and we have experienced great results if people are open to new paths.

Before you start, it is a good idea to recall some important understanding about your company.

- What is your long-term vision?
- Who are your customers?
- What problem are you solving for your customers?
- Where do your customers struggle today?
- Where do you struggle today?

We have observed on many occasion how opportunities emerge based on the unique history, positioning and talent of companies. It is their unique characteristics that define their unique strengths, which delivers them competitive advantages over other organizations striving to achieve similar goals. This is what you should leverage in the age of artificial intelligence. Play to your strengths, they have been the source of your success.

Let's now look at two methods to start exploring your AI opportunity. We will start with the most conservative one, the evolutionary approach. It turns out to be the simpler of the two to execute, because all the building blocks are in place and proven by many companies. In essence it enhances your existing products and processes. Then there is the radical approach, likely to disrupt your current business approach and offering.

The evolutionary approach	The radical approach
Improving existing offerings and prcesses	Discovering disruptire business scenarios

Fig. 10.1 Two approaches to discover AI your opportunity — evolutionary and radical

We will build on our prior case study of Tesla to illustrate some of the concepts but also add a lot of other examples for your reference. We have seen that they can be applied to almost any business out there, irrespective of industry.

The Evolutionary Approach

The accelerated development of Artificial Intelligence in recent years has produced a number of solid use cases. There areas have undergone massive research, testing, application in many practical areas at large scale and continue to improve with further usages, as is natural to AI capabilities. The big four platform providers IBM, Google, Amazon and Microsoft are likely to provide AI capabilities in the form of cloud platforms. Here you utilize AI capabilities as-a-service without having to download, install and configure Artificial Intelligence libraries, let alone develop your own. You can easily work with test data and run some experiments before you scale your solutions.

Let's take IBM Watson, which offers the following areas of ready-to-use capabilities (as of June 2017) as a service:

- **Conversation** — Add a natural language interface to your application to automate interactions with your end users.
- **Document conversion** — The IBM Watson™ Document conversion service converts a single HTML, PDF, or Microsoft Word™ document into a normalized HTML, plain text, or a set of JSON-formatted answer units that can be used with other Watson services.
- **Language translation** — Dynamically translate news, patents, or conversational documents. Instantly publish content in multiple languages.
- **Natural language classifiers** — The Natural Language Classifier service applies cognitive computing techniques to return the best matching classes for a sentence or phrase.
- **Natural language understanding** — Analyze text to extract meta-data from content such as concepts, entities, keywords, categories, sentiment, emotion, relations, semantic roles, using natural language understanding.
- **Personality insights** — Watson Personality Insights: Personality Insights derives insights from transactional and social media data to identify psychological traits which determine purchase decisions, intent and behavioral trait.
- **Retrieve and rank** — The IBM Watson Retrieve and Rank service helps users find the most relevant information for their query by using a combination of search and machine learning algorithms to detect "signals" in the data.
- **Tone analyzer** — Humans exhibit a range of 'tones' such as joy, sadness, anger, and agreeableness, in daily communications. Tone Analyzer uses cognitive linguistic analysis to identify a variety of tones at both the sentence and document level. This insight can then be used/applied to refine and improve communications.
- **Speech to text** — The Speech to Text service converts the human voice into written word. It can be used anywhere there is a need to bridge the gap between the spoken word and their written form, including voice control of embedded systems,

transcription of meetings and conference calls, and dictation of email and notes.

- **Text to speech** — The Text to Speech service processes text and natural language to generate synthesized audio output complete with appropriate cadence and intonation.
- **Visual recognition** — Find meaning in visual content! Analyze images for scenes, objects, faces, and other content.
- **Discovery** — Add a cognitive search and content analytics engine to applications to identify patterns, trends and actionable insights that drive better decision-making.

These capabilities are available to you instantly. Now back to our example of Tesla. Their built-in cameras are capable of constantly taking pictures and videos. AI can be trained to understand those pictures. What is observed in the picture? Are there any obstacles on the road? For AI to learn computer vision, it must be fed with training data. Based on the training data and feedback on correct interpretation, the AI can learn to identify objects more precisely than humans can. Take 3D simulators. These are used to train AI faster. Over time the AI-based algorithm improves and can be made available to more cars.

Let's look at another example in the areas of customer interaction. Let's say your website offers a support chat to assist and guide customers on finding the right information or contact. This can be based on AI capabilities. Here the training data can consist of responses from well-delivered customer interactions. These can be used to train the AI on how to communicate well. Once the AI takes over, the confidence level of a given customer interaction decides whether a human support agent jumps into the conversation, or whether the AI completes the conversation. Just try it, it is a fun experiment. And AI can speak several languages.

Six Pillars of the Evolutionary Approach

The evolutionary approach for Artificial Intelligence focuses on evolving your business by making existing products, service and business processes better. In the evolutionary approach we often observe that AI can carry out tasks cheaper than traditional means. To discover the right opportunity, it is best to start with your existing business practice and products. In our discussions with companies, we have worked on six fields to analyze the status-quo and uncover potential areas of AI improvements:

Your company data stream	Your software
What data streams are available? Can they be optimized and used in more intelligent ways?	What software suites and applications are you using? How can they be made more intelligent?
Your processes	**Your interaction**
Review your processes, discover friction and losses and how they can be more intelligent.	What interactions do you have with your team, your partners and customers?
Your products	**Your Services**
Review your products and offerings to see how artificial intelligence can help them be more cost effective and provide more value.	What services are you offering? How can they benefit from intelligence?

Fig. 10.2 Six pillars of evolutionary approach discovery

Let us provide some insight on tackling each area and devise the right application for your organization.

Your Company Data Streams

Big Data has shaken up a lot of organizations and created an awareness for the value of data. Although most companies we have worked with have engaged in Big Data projects, we are surprised to find that most organization are not aware of the plethora of data they operate on, where the data is stored and what costs are involved in creating, storing, and managing the data. The quality of the data is often in 'suboptimal shape', to put it nicely. When engaging with companies we often start by listing the data sources inside the company and the storage. To name a few: E-Mails, customer data, financial data, suppliers data, interaction data, transaction data, sales data, product lifecycle data. Thereafter we examine the data being used or generated in your products and service. Often all this data is stored in databases, data warehouses or proprietary software systems. Lastly we think of new data sets that can be created by adding additional data sources or engaging sensors.

In correspondence with this practice, we then carry out two exercises for each data set, with the goal of understanding the impact. We carry this out with a diverse group of experts from the company. If possible — we recommend including a data scientist. Furthermore, do not forget to consider outside data sources that can be used to augment and enhance your company data. Here are the two exercises that you should conduct:

- What decisions can be derived from each data set - this focuses on the primary usage of the data, but we also brainstorm how else this data could be used.
- What efforts are needed to create, store and process each data set — here we look at the total cost on how this data is being managed and used. Companies are often not aware how much effort is behind creating their own data flows.

Now let's apply this using a tool that all organizations have at their disposal: your customers data. Think of your own organization. Are you happy with your customer data? Is it good quality and are you utilizing it effectively? Our findings conclude that for most organizations this is a huge potential to be exploited. Here are some examples of questions you might ask:

- Who are your top customers and what are their characteristics?
- Which customers are on their way to becoming top customers

and what are the patterns that define this?
- What is the next predicted purchase for this customer and what are the signs indicating this?
- What customers are in the process of leaving your company for your competitor and how do you detect this?
- What products are your customers purchasing and what products are reaching the end of their lifecycle soon?
- Based on the communication and behavior, how happy are customers with your products and services, how loyal are they to your brand?

By crunching the numbers, understanding the patterns and predicting the trends your team of experts can figure out the answer to these questions. The data scientist can then utilize these insights and develop complex algorithms for your programming team to input into algorithms. It is even beneficial to carry this out manually as it can help you predict behavior and allows you to make better decision on product management, marketing, customer support, and many areas that consume most of your company's budget. Most notably, this is where artificial intelligence can really make a difference. Neural networks are good at identifying complex patterns and making good predictions. AI is a great tool for helping your company understand your data streams, make sense of them, and allow you to make better decisions based on this data. We recommend running experiments on some of the data with the most leverage. By running those experiments you will learn how to engage with artificial intelligence as well as the pitfalls in quality of your data, confidence level, training the neural networks and you build up a new competence in an area, which will be a critical competitive factor in your company's future.

Your role in all of this will be to identify the right areas where it makes sense to engage and develop your AI project. Then to find the right AI tools to help you recognize and understand the data, and finally, perhaps most importantly, your job is to find the right business model to act upon this, as we have learned in the first section of the second part of this book.

Your Software

Wherever you find data, software is not far. It is used to manage the data flows, to store the data, and to act upon it. Therefore another approach to discovering your AI potential is to review your software. You can do so by making a list of the software that is deployed in your organization. Often your software acts upon the same data, so it makes sense to also review what software is working together on data sets. Again ask yourself some question on each of the software you are using:

- What data is your software creating or acting upon and what decisions do you take on that data?
- What additional decisions would you like to take based on the data?
- What efforts are needed to derive those decision and how can they be taken more intelligently?

Then rank the software and corresponding data by most impact both in terms of cost savings and also in terms of new insights and better decision to be taken.

Let's take your HR software as an example. It lists your employees, their performance and feedback, their time spent working, vacationing, just to name a few. So what are the questions should you ask yourself?

- Am I hiring the right people?
- Which people are going to leave soon?
- How is the motivation in my organization?
- How are the managers performing?
- What teams are creating most value and why?

Again, these are just a few examples. Your role in this will be to identify the right areas for your organization to engage, generate the data sources, enable AI to understand the patterns and find ways to engage that provide the most value to your organization. A number of software systems are being enhanced by AI from its creators or new AI based tools are available. It makes sense to do some research before you engage.

Your Processes

Most of your organization is likely to work on business processes on a daily, weekly, monthly, quarterly, or yearly basis. Make a list of your business processes, both primary and secondary. By now patterns should emerge as you dive deeper through each section.

Ask yourselves the following questions for each process:

- What decisions are you taking based on this process?
- How much effort is it to conduct the process, what are the total costs?
- Could this process be automated? Could parts of the process be automated?
- What insights could be taken on the data generated in the process?

Now rank your findings in terms of business impact. What are the biggest problems you would like to solve? Where do you expect to earn the greatest gain? Where can you significantly save costs? What is your ability to execute on these areas? There is no standard answer to these questions, we recognize that this is quite individual to each organization and this is your value in an artificial intelligence world — to translate the new capabilities into your business.

Another area is to look for modern software suites that are business process focused. Companies such as Atlassian, Salesforce, SAP, IBM, Adobe are only a few well-known players in the market. A whole new ecosystem of enterprise software has AI-capabilities built in right from the start.

Fig. 10.3 TopBots Enterprise AI landscape 2017

Your Interactions

AI is showing promising results in enhancing human and company relations, such as translating languages in real time from human to machine (bot). As well as customer service automation and bot-to-bot interactions (for business-to-business commerce). This is a prosperous area for your business to benefit from as it is expanding rapidly. List all your company's interactions and ask yourself the following questions:

- What decisions are being taken according to the interaction?
- How much effort is it to engage in these interactions and what are the total costs?
- Could part of the interaction be automated?

Again rank your findings in order of importance to your organization and identify the areas of biggest value. Note that interactions based on text, speech and image have been among the early areas of progress for AI. So, there are a lot of services and software solutions available to plug-into your enterprise to assist in these processes.

One example are chatbots or voice assistants like Amazon Echo, Apple Siri or Google Home. These AI-based conversational services allow you to automate parts of your customer interactions and thereby provide a personalized interface with a human-like interaction. Voice assistant services can be deployed through the available devices and chatbots can be integrated directly into your digital offerings or integrated into popular messenger platforms like Facebook Messenger, or WhatsApp.

The problem with this is that we often find that their experience is not perfect. Thus it often makes sense to deploy a combination of machine and human intelligence in the solution. If you take chatbots for example, the solutions can be a combination of machine and human where the machine introduces the chat and asks and responds to questions where it has a high confidence level. Questions more complex in nature are handed over to humans to carry on the interaction. This unburdening of customer support people can result in significant cost savings.

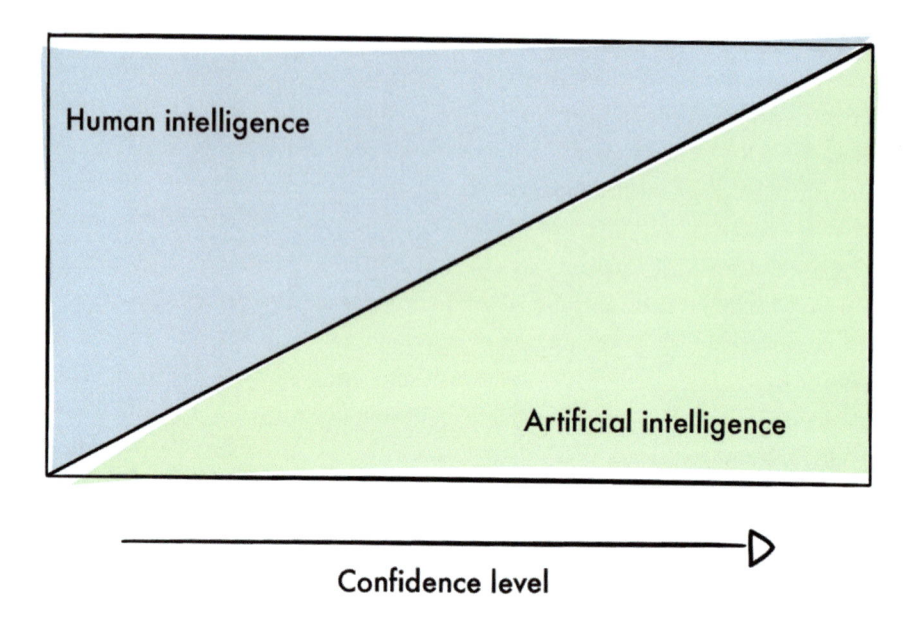

Fig. 10.4 Gradual takeover by AI from humans as the confidence level increases

Above is a model of joint deployment of human intelligence with artificial intelligence, where AI takes on more workload, as the confidence level increases.

Your Products & Services

The last area we will look at are your products and services. You can build AI into your products and service, because AI can get the job done cheaper meaning cost-savings for you, or because it can deliver new capabilities to your customers and ultimately increase the value of your products and services.

How AI can support your products and services can be based on simply adding mature AI areas, such as speech recognition, text to speech, conversation, image recognition. Look to the current set of capabilities of major AI platforms by IBM, Google, Amazon, Microsoft or look at the AI software landscape for capabilities to add to your products. You can achieve some significant results in making interfaces nice, more intelligent, adding better support capabilities and faster results for your users. Because of the proven areas, there is a lower development and integration time and it is easy to prototype and test the benefits before deploying the solution. Be aware though, that your competitors are also working on such solutions and because you are using standard AI services, it might not result in a long-term differentiation from your competitors.

As we covered in the first part of this book, an example of this might be the Netflix video service that created an Amazon Echo Skill that allows people to control their Netflix experience by simply using their voice. "Alexa, I want to watch my favorite Netflix series." This can result in a complex multi-step service, which makes the experience so much more compelling. Amazon Echo turns the TV on, loads Netflix, tunes into the right person based on the voice profile, selects the favorite series, and launches the next episode. If you have deployed some smart-home solutions, it can also automatically lower the window blinds and turn down the lights without additional commands.

A more beneficial approach is to marry the USPs of your product and brand with AI capabilities. An excellent example of this is Amazon optimizing product suggestions based on AI or Google Translate improving their translation services based on Machine Learning or BMW offering smoother braking algorithms. Take your existing products and services and make them even better in areas that differentiate. To achieve this, you make lists in 3 areas:

1. The use cases and values delivered
2. The product / service features
3. Your unique area of expertise and differentiation from the competition

For each item, list the data flows and think of how they can be made more intelligent and cost-effective. From this, you should also brainstorm what are new areas where you can deliver valuable use cases and offer new features. We recommend creating a systems map, listing on the left the stakeholders involved and on the right the end result. In order to visualize the process and data flows you draw boxes around them. Mark the areas where AI can help optimize the process. This will reveal what data is needed and how to get it— for example by deploying new sensors. This is not the last step though, you can deploy AI libraries in the right places to offer AI services and self-learning algorithms. You have to train these AI systems so think of training scenarios and getting training data. Then you go on extensive training phase to develop and train the artificial intelligence before deploying to your products and services.

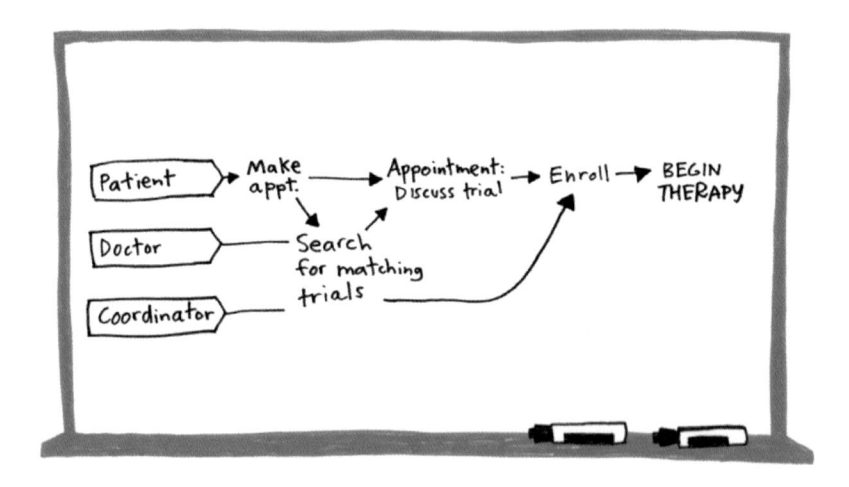

Fig. 10.5 Example of a systems map from Google Venture SPRINT book

Reflecting again on the Salesforce CRM software. The company's strength of offering software-as-a-service and combining many customer facing tasks in a unified platform offering was the basis for adding new value through their Artificial Intelligence offering' Einstein.' Traditional Salesforce CRM was good at ranking top customers based on revenue data for example, but Einstein allows you to understand why the customers are top. What are the characteristics of top customers, what other customers are on their path to become top customers? When will these customers buy again? Here Salesforce played on their differentiating strengths and they have made CRM much more intelligent and beneficial to their users. The result of this is it allows them to charge a premium. It is still early days, but we can foresee a time where companies will not buy a CRM system that is not based on artificial intelligence. It will be too costly for the companies, because business operations and decisions will not be as optimized as those where the companies deploy intelligent CRM systems.

This kind of Artificial Intelligence requires a deeper engagement by employees working on the core products and services. You also need to delve into unproven ways, which are likely to be more costly and risky. But the reward can be a higher differentiation of your products and services. Often this requires senior management commitment and a strong vision, if you wish to benefit from these capabilities early. If you are not an early mover, don't worry— your competition will drive you to this space very soon, as we are entering the era of artificial intelligence.

Going through this process helps you identify areas where you can gain most benefits from AI. They are easy to identify and engage with and will kick off your AI journey. However, they are not sufficient to exploit the maximum benefits for your organization. Now we have explored this approach let's explore an entirely different approach to identifying your AI potential.

The Radical Approach— Discovering Disrupting Business Scenarios

So here comes the fun part… for some. How do you take your business to the next level with Artificial Intelligence — how do you build the next multi-billion business? While all this sounds exciting, not all enjoy this part, especially the successful multinationals that have evolved over time. They have developed mechanisms to optimize and keep the status-quo. In our work with these enterprises, we have found that there is an initial interest in Artificial Intelligence, but then there is a tendency to push it out into the future, or to find ways in arguing that this will never be really relevant, or will not work with their customers. This happens once the initial interest wears out. To overcome this natural defense of change, we have developed a simple method to help overcome the fears, doubts, and uncertainties.

We have found that in order to play to the full potential of artificial intelligence it is important to go beyond the limitations that artificial intelligence has today. It is those limitations where most people's doubts fester and the uncertainty of costs and quality limit the execution power. In addition, it is the fear of jobs, the power of robots, the social impact that limits the drive towards leveraging AI. Our method for overcoming this is to envision ourselves ten years into the future. Let's try this exercise now. Imagine yourself ten years in the future. What do you picture? AI will have obviously improved significantly and its combination with advancements in other areas such as robotics and taken alone will give you capabilities unthinkable of today. We chose ten years because it is just far enough to be tangible without some apocalyptic scenarios. In doing this, it offers significant chance and takes you of your current limitations. Take yourself out of your current position and time and look at the big picture. It took just ten years for the iPhone to radically change the way people interact with digital services.

We call this moment, the time of "perfect AI". This is because regardless of how far AI will be in ten years and what other factors or technologies will play a role, it is far out enough of people's mindset to dive head first into a space that is so fundamentally different that it forces new thinking to open up. Experts accept that perfect AI could be a reality. It is important not to be bogged down by today's limitations and lack of imagination.

So we pose the following question:

"If there is perfect AI in ten years, what is the role of your company and what will your business model look like?"

We intentionally pose the question in two parts. We start with an opening scene. There is likely to be powerful and intelligent software and totally new interactions. Data and processing power will be ubiquitous, machines will have found a perfect way to interact with humans. Humans will have started to trust machines for some critical things in their lives. Now we will describe one of our experiences exploring this question with a firm via a workshop on the "picture of the future". The picture of the future can contain several likely scenes that are scribbled by the team. Obviously, the quality of the scribbles does not matter. Then we enhance the picture with Post-It notes in several colors representing where AI is used (which is often hidden). This helps the team express interesting areas and gives you a visual aid where innovation is possible.

Based on this picture of the future, we worked on possible scenarios describing the role of the firm in this picture of the future. This is a vital step in understanding the scope of the change. Will you be the sole supplier, will you deliver an integrated use case, or rather just some core components? What will your relationship with other players be and how will you interact with your customers and who will those customers be? As a whole, what will the total ecosystem look like? What will be your role in the game? Again, you should focus on your strengths and potential differentiating factors.

The final step is to consider business models that monetize the value you propose. Here you can visit the areas where AI will play in the picture of the future — don't forget you are in the ultimate all perfect AI scenario, so don't worry about any shortcomings you see today. What are the resources needed? How big is the customer value? What are potential alternative solutions and players delivering that service? We usually spend extensive time discussing these elements with companies to help them better understand their role, as well as new potential business models and threats. Do you sell the car? Are you an investment vehicle for people who buy the car to rent it out so that it will make money by delivering services for others? Are you provider of data, predicting where people will be and what services they want? Are you monetizing on the data or services? These are just some examples to illustrate how future business models based on AI might be very different.

Before you rip up your whole business model remember that this is just an exercise and you don't have to change your vision, mission and entire organization just yet. The real intention here is to help you think far enough and to understand possible scenarios, before identifying the first step. So based on your favorite scenario, you break down the vision and think of what is the first, most logical step in making it happen. This is where you should start. Identify and describe the first step in detail. Often this first step is not too far out, and is both conceivable and achievable. It is easy to understand, discuss and test with users to ensure you are on right path.

This is best illustrated with an example. Let's say you are an automobile manufacturer (OEM) and you are designing and producing cars. How can artificial intelligence disrupt your business? Obviously your business is influenced by three major trends in 2017. Firstly, the sharing economy where people are less inclined to purchase cars vs. renting on demand. The second impact is the move to e-mobility. The car's system changes fundamentally from motor and transmission-based approaches to much simpler battery-powered e-motors. In addition, the move to autonomous vehicles require you to build completely new components and software into your vehicles. And here is where we see the era of artificial intelligence coming into play. Again we ask the question: "So if there were perfect AI in 10 years, what would your business model look like and what is the role of your company?".

You can find inspiration all around you. Science fiction movies are often a good source. In a perfect world of artificial intelligence, cars might become cheaper to build. Robots might build the robots that will build cars in smart factories. Smart materials might be more flexible with built-in sensors. Smart mobility grids will allow the users and vehicles to plug-into a network of services and mobility options. Vehicles might be living spaces allowing you to play, conduct meetings and even take meals during transportation times. You might be able to seamlessly switch from one mode of transportation to another to reach your destination. For customers the biggest choice might be whether to take a self-flying drone or a ground-based vehicle. Drones might be cheaper due to simpler technology. Flying in the air can pose less complex situations than cars driving on the roads with so many distractions and obstacles. Drones might be a lot quicker, as they can take direct paths. This is an example of how to develop a picture of the future. Of course your experts, together with some external inspiration will produce a vast array of innovative scenarios to base your thinking on.

As a next step you will define the role you wish to play in this scenario. The role you will play in the future will be based on your history, what you are good at, and your area of differentiation. You might still manufacture and supply cars, if this is your key area of competence. Or will you just supply parts or designs to other players? Will you build autonomous drones? Do you offer sharing services? Will you program the network that the cars run on? Will you provide services or build an ecosystem of 3rd party service providers? It makes sense to list and discuss each of the options. Then you can discuss your business model.

Where AI will make a decisive different to you will become clear based on the discussion accumulated from these various areas. From this, you can start your engagement and experiments with artificial intelligence. You will learn to work with the technology, to build awareness and knowledge in your organization, and you will explore a journey with a bigger goal in mind.

11. Introducing the AI&U Canvas – Your AI Strategy Blueprint

Once you have arrived at one or more business ideas for innovation with AI, it is a good practice to map out the various parameters of that idea in a structured manner. This will make it easier to examine various aspects of the idea and the correlations between them. It serves as an excellent document for objectively discussing and refining the concept with other stakeholders. There are various methodologies for doing this. Below we have developed our own chart to do this, the "AI&U Canvas," derived from the classic Business Canvas template, by Alex Osterwalder. Once filled out with the parameters of your business model for AI, the AI&U Canvas becomes your AI strategy blueprint. The AI&U Canvas consists of 8 fields defining the components of your AI solution. Three fields on the right (green) lists customer facing areas for the solution. Three fields on the left (blue) capture internal considerations for creating the solution. Two fields in the center (yellow) capture the value. Your AI solution fields are:

- Customers (and stakeholders)
- Interactions (with customers)
- Value Proposition (for customers)
- Data Sources and Sensors (for AI)
- AI Services
- Ecosystem Partners
- AI Value Add
- Business Benefits

AI&U – Translating Artificial Intelligence into Business

AI Project: **Date:** **Version:**

Ecosystem Partners
All ecosystem partners needed for creation, operation and service of the solution

Examples:
- AI platform - e.g. Google, IBM, Microsoft or Amazon
- AI neural network set up, Deep Learning training and maintenance
- Data sourcing

AI Services
All AI services needed for the solution

Examples:
- Speech recognition
- Object recognition
- Scene description

Data Sources & Sensors
All sources of data used for AI with sensors, if needed

Examples:
- Medical history and clinical data for healthcare and sensors
- Income, investments, expenses etc. i.e for Tax consultants
- Temperature, humidity, rain, soil etc. for agriculture and sensors

Business Benefits
Benefits to the business as a result of the solution

Examples:
- Reduction of human power - lower cost
- Higher customer satisfaction and trust
- Higher quality of service - more competitive

AI Value Add
Value added to the solution due to the use of AI

Examples:
- Direct speech input - no typing
- Automatic recognition of critical situations
- Higher accuracy than a human expert

AI&U™ Canvas

Interactions
All interactions with customers with the solution

Examples:
- Presentations
- Sales process
- Writing proposals
- Customer service calls

Value Propositions
Value offered to customers by the solution

Examples:
- Better ease of use
- Higher personalization
- Proactive and responsive

Customers
All customers (internal and external) served by the solution

Examples:
- Internal customers
- External customer segments
- End customers
- Channel customers

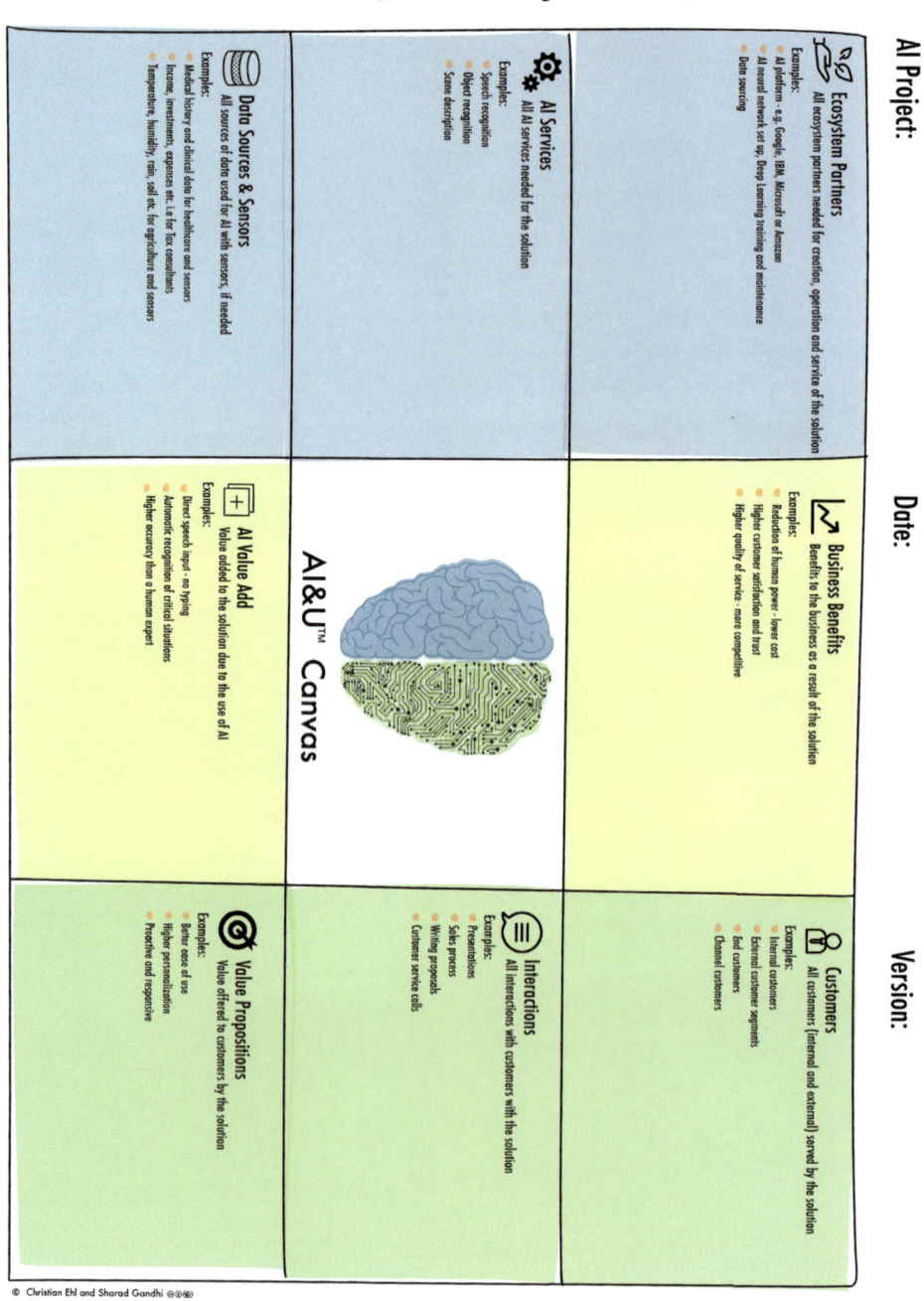

© Christian Ehl and Sharad Gandhi

Fig. 11.1 AI&U Canvas summarizes your AI strategy

These components are essential to understand any AI-based solution. Here is the structure of a typical AI solution.

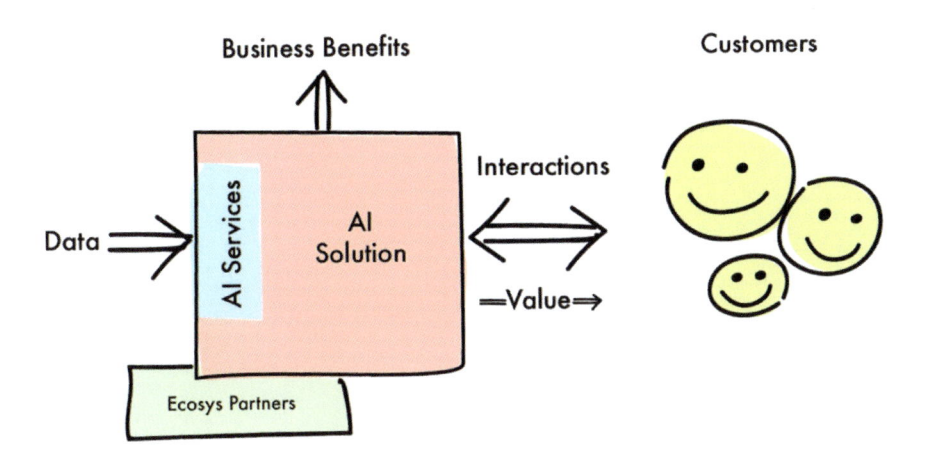

Fig. 11.2 Anatomy of a typical AI solution

Every AI solution converts **data** from the real world — speech, sounds, images etc. – into value for the customer (Fig. 11.2). An AI solution has **interactions** with (internal and/or external, one or more) **customers**, delivering **business value**. A satisfied and happy customer is characterized as one who benefits from the solution if the value provided meets or exceeds their needs. AI solutions typically can benefit from the support of certain **AI services**, like speech recognition, object recognition, or face recognition. These are basic AI services typically licensed from external companies. These services make it much easier and faster to build the AI solution delivering customer value. Often there is a collaborative need from other companies, called **Ecosystem Partners**, to enable the entire solution to work. These are AI platform providers such as Google, Amazon, Microsoft, IBM, or specialized providers for Deep Learning. **AI value add** in the solution stems from the integration of AI. In the end the total solution must deliver overall **business benefits** for your business — in terms of you winning new customers, generating higher revenues, reducing costs, or enabling expansion to other geographies.

These highlighted components (above) are identified and filled out in the AI&U Canvas fields providing an excellent documentation of the AI solution and all its major components. We recommend filling out the fields in the order shown below as objectively as possible — possibly as a collaborative effort by the AI team.

You can download your copy of the canvas at the AI&U website www.ai-u.org.

1. Customers and Stakeholders
Write down all customers (internal and external) served by the solution. You can also add their key needs.

Examples:
- Internal customers
- Stakeholders
- External customer segments
- End customers
- Channel customers

2. Interactions
List the ways in which customer interact with the solution — especially where the AI elements come into play.

Examples:
- Presentations
- Sales process
- Writing proposals
- Customer service calls

3. Value Propositions
Specify the value your solution offers to each of your customer segments. Keep in mind that this is not a list of your solution features.

Examples:
- Improve Ease of Use

- Higher personalization
- Proactive and responsive

4. Data Sources & Sensors

List all sources of data used for AI. If needed for the data, name the sensors. Remember that AI transforms data into value offered to customers, hence data is the raw material for AI.

Examples:
- Medical history and clinical data for healthcare + sensors
- Income, investments, expenses, etc. for tax consultants
- Temperature, humidity, rain, soil, etc. for agriculture + sensors

5. AI Services

List AI services needed for the solution. These services are typically licensed from third parties. If known, name the provider.

Examples:
- Speech recognition
- Object recognition
- Scene description

6. Ecosystem Partners

List all ecosystem partners needed for creation, operation and service of the solution.

Examples:
- AI Platform — e.g. Google, IBM, Microsoft or Amazon
- AI Neural-network set up, Deep Learning training and maintenance
- Data sourcing

7. AI Value Add

Value added to the solution due to use of AI. This is an indicator of the incremental value that AI exclusively brings to your solution. Some benefits can be realized internally, by automating processes, without the customer noticing any change themselves.

Examples:

- Direct speech input — no typing
- Automatic recognition of critical situations
- Higher accuracy than a human expert

8. Business Benefits

Benefits for your business as a result of the solution. These are essentially benefits to your firm, with a financial and strategic impact, by offering an AI based solution.

Examples:
- Reduction of human-power - lower cost
- Higher customer satisfaction and trust
- Higher quality of service — more competitive

12. Developing Your AI Strategy

The first step in developing an AI solution is to discover and finalize a creative idea at the core of your solution. You may have devised several ideas, therefore you need to have a process for short listing the most viable idea and honing in on it. We recommend carrying out customer interviews and experiments that validate your assumptions and prevent you from delving into areas that are not relevant. We often use the method of Google Venture's Sprints method which brings together a team of 5-8 people to find answers to big problems in just 5 days, and validates the answers with real customers. By doing this in only 5 days, it ensures the team focuses only on the important aspects, and ensures nobody becomes too attached to the solution before it is validated or discarded. If you are using a cloud-based AI service, you can also add developers to your SPRINT team, which will help you to develop a real and functioning prototype. Running these such experiments is critical to making fast progress.

Now you need to develop a strategy around the creative AI idea. Since AI is a new technology, you may find that for most companies, multiple iterations of strategic reviews and management approval are needed to get a go ahead. This is not only because AI is new in nature, but also management may not have a clear idea on the impact on the bottom line. Jeff Bezos, CEO of Amazon, says that many benefits resulting from AI are internal to the company, meaning a reduction of costs may not be immediately obvious. The value to customers can sometimes be translated in the form of significantly better personalization, higher accuracy, and ease of use.

As with any project, an AI project must start with absolute clarity on two areas defining the strategy:

- **Value Proposition (VP):** What new value are you offering to your customer segments? Which customer segments are you addressing and what are their needs? Will your new value offering better satisfy customer needs?
- **Business Model (BM):** How will your business benefit from the new offering? How will you monetize this value proposition? This involves a clear understanding of the sources of your revenue, costs, partners, and interactions involved.

These two areas describe the total value of your AI project to customers and to your business overall. You will find that these two areas are non-trivial and often need the highest quality of attention and time. The rest is a matter of implementation.

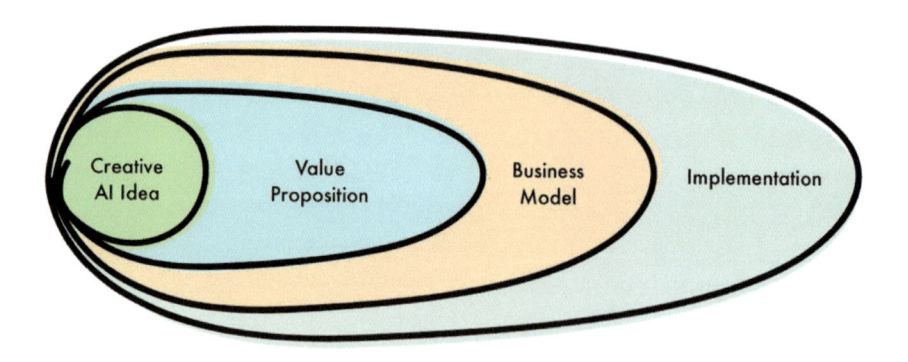

Fig. 12.1 Developing your AI strategy — from the creative idea to implementation

Articulating a VP for AI-based projects requires an excellent understanding of the new capabilities that are enabled by AI today and in the near future. The low hanging fruits of AI capabilities are speech input, computer vision input, people and face recognition, image and object recognition, and scene description. New capabilities are evolving every day. The core VP for your business will be centered around a creative AI idea that leverages one or more new capabilities of AI, in order to deliver new and unique value to your customers. The BM converts the VP into a profitable business. Development and approval of a solid VP and BM for AI solutions is the first and most important step for AI. Since AI is a new technology with benefits that are often not well understood, this often takes much longer than expected. The availability of AI services and platforms help in implementation of the solution. The AI&U canvas is useful in capturing all critical elements of your solution, and allowing you and other decision makers to discuss, and form a consensus.

New Skills and Competencies for AI Projects

As with any project, success depends on a number of fundamental skills and efficient processes. These are areas such as strategy articulation, getting project approval, planning, project management, and customer validation. However, AI projects also require a number of new skills:

- Understanding of new AI capabilities
- Knowledge of available AI services
- Working with AI platforms
- Accessing data sources and sensors
- Machine Learning
- Neural Network setup, configuration and optimization
- AI - Human interfacing

AI has the power to radically transform a company's entire approach to products and way they are offered. This requires a very open mindset regarding the company's business objectives and core strengths. It is vital that the company strategy and product planning team have people with excellent insights into the potential of AI, and new capabilities enabled by it. External expertise can be of big help for guidance on the maturity and applicability of new AI to company goals.

When it comes to AI basic services, it makes little sense to develop internal expertise on AI services, like speech recognition, translation, or smart mail response services, as these basic services are available as open source, or from multiple vendors. You just need to pick the service that best matches your needs. Major AI players like Google, Amazon, IBM, and

Microsoft offer platforms for development of AI projects. These platforms offer many AI services, tools and consulting services, which can significantly cut down prototyping and customer validation time. AI specialist companies can be used for specific areas such as, setting up neural networks, training the AI system, and collection of data.

The design of AI systems needs a good understanding of the data needed by the AI systems for reliable operation, as data is their raw material for AI systems. Machine learning and neural networks form the core of any AI system. Machine learning needs validated data sets for training the neural network as well as reliable, up-to-date and good quality data as input for decision making. Some of the required data originate from dedicated sensors. Data scientists are the specialists in this area, and must be a part of the AI team, since they ensure that the data is appropriate, neural networks are setup and optimized, and the network is trained.

Humans have learned how to interact and communicate with humans over thousands of years. We have learned to interface with one another. AI is learning to mimic humans in these specific areas but interfacing AI with humans remains far from trivial. Even the simplest AI devices such as, the Amazon Echo or Google Assistant need excellent interfacing with humans, making the communication feel natural and human-like. I am more likely to use the Echo when my communication with it is so natural that I can hardly differentiate the experience from that of interacting with a human.

Organization — With a Data and AI Mindset

Machines of the industrial revolution performed repetitive mechanical tasks at a higher level of accuracy, reliability, productivity, and cost efficiency than humans, and as a result, eliminated many jobs. Similarly repetitive information jobs such as granting approval for opening a bank account, granting loans, filling out forms, providing information, transferring information from A to B, call centers etc. will be increasingly delegated to AI, making many jobs which humans perform today redundant. The new job roles in organizations will be expected to leverage data and the power of AI in order to accomplish higher level task.

An HR specialist of tomorrow will automatically have AI seek out the best candidates to hire and set up the interviews with hiring managers. The HR role will shift to a higher level — salary negotiations and ensuring fast integration of the new hire. When I was first hired, mature PC and mobile skills were a basic requirement. The new hires of the future will be required to be AI-aware and AI-friendly, just as we are PC- and mobile-friendly in our current work.

There will be new AI tools used as a standard practice – such as Einstein from Salesforce.com - which will provide a sales or marketing person with much richer information. For example, analysis and prediction by AI about a customer's intent, and for suggesting alternatives on how and when to best submit sales proposals.

Most jobs will be transformed, making Change Management one of the biggest challenges for companies seeking success in the AI age. Beyond changing individual job roles and skills, the organization of employees will also need a fresh approach. The exact nature of the transformation is not easy to predict, as it will depend on the nature of business, country of operation, and company culture.

Alex Osterwalder & Yves Pigneur, the authors of the popular books, Business Model Generation and Value Proposition Design, have made a compelling case for appointing a Chief Entrepreneur in a company to focus on the future of the company while the CEO focuses on the present. (http://blog.strategyzer.com/posts/2017/7/11/an-open-letter-to-ceos)

13. Outlook

So, where do you think all of this is going to lead your company and you as an individual? From a year ago when we first began thinking about this book up until the very completion of it, the news and buzz surrounding AI has intensified even further. So has the availability of services, the breadth of the ecosystem and the sheer amount of ongoing AI projects. This paves the road towards an accelerated future.

In this book, we have focused on what's possible today, why companies should engage now and what are good approaches and useful areas. From this we have seen how AI technologies are destined to become or to be integrated into every part, from the software you use to managing data sources to optimizing your processes to your products and services, AI is becoming pervasive. AI will help you make better decisions and become a key ingredient in your business activities. Based on this, we are likely to see quite an increase in productivity in combination with other technologies like robotics, sensors, materials, computing and connectivity. We may even witness an exponential increase in productivity, where AI plays a key role. Soon machines create the factories. Tesla is already working on this today. The question is, what will happen then, and what does that mean for your business?

"The future is more predictable than you think" are famous words uttered by Google's chief futurist Ray Kurzweil. And this holds true for a lot of technology. We can imagine what autonomous vehicles will be like, how voice computing will change the user experience and interfaces and how human sensors will give us more insight into our health, to name a few areas. However, the predictions for artificial intelligence to reach or surpass human level intelligence are difficult to imagine.

With this said, the impact of the technology revolution will be hard to predict. How will it change our lives? What will we do if intelligent machines can do most of the work? What will be the role of humans in a super intelligent world? Will there be states or corporations? In the early days of the Internet, it was not foreseeable where the Internet would take us in such a short period of times. The impact of technology is immensely difficult to predict and we will not even attempt to predict what might happen when super intelligence has arrived. However, we have found a few interesting points of discussion, which we would like to summarize in four scenarios to give you some inspiration of what might happen.

Scenario 1: Productivity Gains Allow Humans to Focus on Being Human

Let's start with a positive scenario. After all, technology provides an unprecedented opportunity to build a brighter and better future. Modern technology, especially AI and robotics, could well lead to monumental increases in productivity. This could extend to making it easier to feed the growing world population, improve health, longevity, quality of water and food. It may even enable a framework for basic income for all. However, this would require us to rethink our political and social systems and the purpose of humans, as most of the issues and developments happen on a global scale.

Scenario 2: Inequality is on the Rise

While the advancements in artificial intelligence enable high productivity, this also translates as wealth for its creators which can cause economic inequality. Those not leading the development in AI have less chance to compete. The health and longevity of a few improve significantly, while the rest of the population falls behind and can hardly catch up again. This leads to extreme instability and suffering with social unrest.

Scenario 3: AI Warfare and Terrorism

We are beginning to see the negative sides of technology, with automated drones and intelligent cyber warfare being exploited by people with evil or destructive intentions. As the machines become extremely powerful and super intelligent, regular defenses might not be sufficient or the good side will always lose, leading to an unstoppable downward spiral. The only way to compete is to use better AI, resulting in a worldwide arms race that consumes most resources.

Scenario 4: The Cyborg vs. Superintelligent Machine

We have evolved as cyborgs for many decades. Everything from electronic hearing aids and cardiac pacemakers to even smartwatches and smartphones have expanded our capabilities of living, problem solving, communicating significantly. As the technology becomes ever more advanced, it can greatly augment human capabilities in our favor. If scientists and companies work on solving the machine brain interface, like Elon Musk's Neuralink is attempting, we might be able to directly tap into super intelligence. Just like the evolution of the neo cortex (the outer part of the brain) this connection would act as an additional layer of our brain, giving us super intelligence while still being human at heart. Some consider this the end of homosapiens. Elon Musk seems to think that is the only way we can keep super intelligence from destroying humans.

No one can forecast these scenarios. The future evolves one step at a time. We believe, that we are all in for an amazing ride with an unclear ending, it has always been that way. But we think that you and your organization should not become too obsessed with these unclear scenarios. You have a job to do today. AI is a promising new technology, that can help you achieve new dimensions in your offerings. It is a welcome opportunity for creating higher customer value and reducing your operational costs. So focus on delivering that today.

Conclusions

We associate many qualities such as love, emotions, creativity, imagination and values with human beings. These differentiate us from all other animals on our planet. One such quality is technology. Humans have the unique ability to understand the laws of nature and develop technologies that set us apart with additional advantages, comforts, productivities, and increase our ability to survive. We humans have developed a vast number of technologies in our history that have radically changed our lifestyles and future. It is these very changes that have allowed us to conquer fatal diseases, create new materials, program genes to create new biological products, tap into the powers of steam, electricity, atom, computing, and the Internet. These have helped in betterment of our lives and increased our life spans. However, like all good things in life, technology also has a flip side. It also creates many undesired side-effects. The new powers of technology have also eradicated huge numbers of animals from the planet, destroyed millions of acres of forest, impacted the climate and environment, killed millions of people in wars and crime, displaced people and their jobs. That is the dualistic nature of technology. AI is the next big technology with an enormous potential to transform our lifestyle for good. We cannot eliminate the negative side effects of mass job displacement, a renewed search for meaning, and the potential dangers to mankind. However, we can be more watchful and have regulatory systems in place to maximize the benefits and minimize the dangers.

We have seen how AI is a natural outcome of technologies for computing, storage, communication, and understanding the human brain, all developed in the last century. AI learning and decision making has many parallels to how the human brain operates. As a result, AI has the ability to take over a number of functions that a human brain normally performs. Decision making is our brain's continual activity. We make decisions all the time ranging from the trivial, such as what to eat for breakfast, to the complex, such as where to invest our money. Now we can delegate a number of these decisions to AI and, in the process, simplify our lives. AI enables more seamless human interfacing to machines with almost perfect speech and gesture recognition and language recognition and translations. These alone will open up computing technology to a vast number of people who cannot use computing services today. AI can make all the decisions from driving our vehicles to operating the robots safely. And this is just the tip of the AI iceberg.

Throughout this book we have shown how it is possible for any business to harness AI to their advantage in creating new value for their customers with an AI differentiated business. We believe it is best to start right now with strategic planning on how AI can transform your business. To aid you in this journey, we have provided some tools such as the AI&U canvas and processes. Many AI platforms and services are available today to further help in the implementation of your AI based solutions.

One thing is certain. If you want to survive and thrive in the age of artificial intelligence, you must become engaged now and start building AI capabilities. We too are committed to continue our work on AI. We wish to empower individuals such as yourself and organizations like yours to seize this historic opportunity.

We have decided to open source our book and release a web version at www.ai-u.org. This online version is completely free and published under the creative commons code. We will continue to update this version with new insights and case studies as they appear.

We are here to help ignite your AI journey. We hold regular talks and workshops as well as publish many articles on the topic of AI. Sometimes, we engage in AI projects. We wish you all the best on your AI journey and would love to hear about your progress. Please share your thoughts by leaving comments on our website.

May the force be with you — and be aware of the dark side.

Sharad and Christian

Appendix

Sources and Recommended Reading

- **Sapiens - a Brief History of Humankind,** Yuval Noah Harari, https://www.amazon.com/Sapiens-Humankind-Yuval-Noah-Harari/dp/0062316095
- **Homo Deus: A Brief History of Tomorrow,** Yuval Noah Harari, https://www.amazon.com/Homo-Deus-Brief-History-Tomorrow/dp/0062464310
- **Computer,** Wikipedia, https://en.m.wikipedia.org/wiki/Computer
- **Moore's Law,** Wikipedia, https://en.m.wikipedia.org/wiki/Moore's_law
- **Internet,** Wikipedia, https://en.m.wikipedia.org/wiki/Internet
- **Cloud Computing,** Wikipedia, https://en.m.wikipedia.org/wiki/Cloud_computing
- **Application Software,** Wikipedia, https://en.m.wikipedia.org/wiki/Application_software
- **Mobile Apps,** Wikipedia, https://en.m.wikipedia.org/wiki/Mobile_app
- **Internet of Things,** Wikipedia, https://en.m.wikipedia.org/wiki/Internet_of_things
- **Big Data,** Wikipedia, https://en.m.wikipedia.org/wiki/Big_data
- **Robotics,** Wikipedia, https://en.m.wikipedia.org/wiki/Robotics
- **Augmented Reality,** Wikipedia, https://en.m.wikipedia.org/wiki/Augmented_reality
- **Artificial Intelligence,** Wikipedia, https://en.m.wikipedia.org/wiki/Artificial_intelligence
- **A Very Short History Of Artificial Intelligence** (AI), Gill Press, Forbes, Dec 30, 2016, https://www.forbes.com/sites/gilpress/2016/12/30/a-very-short-history-of-artificial-intelligence-ai/#4f32b8e16fba
- **Computing Machinery and Intelligence,** "The Imitation Game", Alan M Turing, 1950, http://www.loebner.net/Prizef/TuringArticle.html
- **The Alan Turing Internet Scrapbook,** The Turing Test 1950, http://www.turing.org.uk/scrapbook/test.html
- **Lisp Machine,** Wikipedia, https://en.m.wikipedia.org/wiki/Lisp_machine

- **The AI Revolution**: The Road to Superintelligence - Tim Urban, Wait But Why, January 22, 2015, http://waitbutwhy.com/2015/01/artificial-intelligence-revolution-1.html http://waitbutwhy.com/2015/01/artificial-intelligence-revolution-2.html
- **Top 10 Hot Artificial Intelligence (AI) Technologies**, Gil Press, Forbes, Jan 23, 2017, http://www.forbes.com/sites/gilpress/2017/01/23/top-10-hot-artificial-intelligence-ai-technologies/#f43612c42def
- **Gartner's Hype Cycle 2016**, Gartner, http://www.gartner.com/newsroom/id/3412017
- **How Artificial Intelligence Will Change Everything**, The Wall Street Journal, March 6, 2017 https://www.wsj.com/articles/how-artificial-intelligence-will-change-everything-1488856320
- **Finally, neural networks that actually work**, Cade Metz, Wired, April 21, 2015, https://www.wired.com/2015/04/jeff-dean/
- **IBM speech recognition is on the verge of superhuman accuracy**, Chris Weller, Business Insider, 9.03.2017, http://www.businessinsider.de/ibm-speech-recognition-almost-super-human-2017-3
- **Deep Learning for Beginners**, Shehzad Noor Taus Priyo, Medium, Feb 28, 2017, https://medium.com/towards-data-science/intro-to-deep-learning-d5caceedcf85
- **A Beginner's Guide to Neural Networks**: Part One, Nehal Udyavar, Medium, March 22, 2017, https://medium.com/towards-data-science/a-beginners-guide-to-neural-networks-b6be0d442fa4
- **A Beginner's Guide to Neural Networks**: Part Two, Nehal Udyavar, Medium, March 27, 2017, https://medium.com/towards-data-science/a-beginners-guide-to-neural-networks-part-two-bd503514c71a
- **Hardware for Deep Learning**, Eugenio Culurciello, Medium, March 23, 2017, https://medium.com/towards-data-science/hardware-for-deep-learning-8d9b03df41a
- **Convolutional Neural Networks for Visual Recognition** (CS231n), Stanford, University, http://cs231n.github.io/neural-networks-1/
- **A.I versus M.D. What happens when diagnosis is automated?** Siddharth Mukherjee, The New Yorker, April 3, 2017, http://www.newyorker.com/magazine/2017/04/03/ai-versus-md

- **Artificial Intelligence is the New Electricity**, Andrew Ng, Stanford University, https://www.youtube.com/watch?v=21EiKfQYZXc
- **Can Self-Driving Cars Ever Really Be Safe?** Shelly Palmer, LinkedIn, https://www.linkedin.com/pulse/can-self-driving-cars-ever-really-safe-shelly-palmer
- **The dark secret at the heart of AI**, Will Knight, MIT Technology Review, April 11, 2017, https://www.technologyreview.com/s/604087/the-dark-secret-at-the-heart-of-ai/
- **Fear of Artificial Intelligence**, Paul Ford, MIT Technology Review, February 11, 2015, https://www.technologyreview.com/s/534871/our-fear-of-artificial-intelligence/
- **Deep learning algorithm diagnoses skin cancer as well as seasoned dermatologists**, Jessica Hall, Jan 25, 2017; https://www.extremetech.com/extreme/243352-deep-learning-algorithm-diagnoses-skin-cancer-seasoned-dermatologists
- **The Race To Build An AI Chip For Everything Just Got Real**, Cade Metz, Wired, April https://www.wired.com/2017/04/race-make-ai-chips-everything-heating-fast/
- **Intro to Deep Learning**, Harini Suresh, MIT 6.S191 Lecture 1, https://www.youtube.com/watch?v=IgSuFYamZas
- **TOPBOTS landscape of artificial intelligence**, Marlene Jia, March 31, 2017, http://www.topbots.com/essential-landscape-overview-enterprise-artificial-intelligence/
- **ai-one and the Machine Learning Landscape**, http://www.ai-one.com/2015/01/12/ai-one-and-the-machine-intelligence-landscape/
- **Jack Ma predicted the emergence of the Robot-CEO**, Crowdholding, https://crowdholding.com/blog/121/robots-work-jack-ma-predicted-the-emergence-of-robot-ceo
- **Tesla is explaining how AI will make its self-driving cars smarter**, Kevin J. Ryan, Inc., https://www.inc.com/kevin-j-ryan/how-tesla-is-using-ai-to-make-self-driving-cars-smarter.html
- **Drones could save farmers millions, study finds**, Christopher Doering, The Des Moines Register, July 21, 2015, http://www.desmoinesregister.com/story/money/agriculture/2015/07/21/drones-farm-savings-agriculture-millions/30486487/
- **The 2016 AI Recap: Startups See Record High In Deals And Funding**, CB Insights, Jan 19, 2017,

https://www.cbinsights.com/blog/artificial-intelligence-startup-funding/

- **Amazon's CEO perfectly explains AI in just two sentences**, April 29, 2017, https://futurism.com/amazon-ceo-perfectly-explains-ai-just-two-sentences/
- **Tesla Information** from Tesla Website, https://www.tesla.com
- **Autonomous Car**, Wikipedia, https://en.wikipedia.org/wiki/Autonomous_car
- **Move over, coders - Physicists will soon rule Silicon Valley**, Cade Metz, Jan 16, 2017 Wired, https://www.wired.com/2017/01/move-coders-physicists-will-soon-rule-silicon-valley/
- **How Salesforce CEO Marc Benioff uses artificial intelligence to end internal politics at meetings (Einstein)**, Julie Bort, Business Insider, May 19, 2017, http://www.businessinsider.de/benioff-uses-ai-to-end-politics-at-staff-meetings-2017-5
- **H&R Block turns to AI to tackle your tax returns**, Sharon Gaudin, Computerworld, Feb 23, 2017, http://www.computerworld.com/article/3173283/artificial-intelligence/hr-block-turns-to-ai-to-tackle-your-tax-return.html
- **"Democratize Artificial Intelligence(AI)"**, Google CEO Sundar Pichai at Google I/O 2017 Sunder Pichai, https://www.youtube.com/watch?v=37ZsZv6OsUY
- **Elon Musk (and 350 Experts) Predict Exactly When Artificial Intelligence Will Overtake Human Intelligence**, Kevin J. Ryan, Inc., June 6, 2017, https://www.inc.com/kevin-j-ryan/elon-musk-and-350-experts-revealed-when-ai-will-overtake-humans.html
- **Would You Feel Safer If Your Self-Driving Car Could Explain Itself?**, George Dvorsky, Gizmodo, June 6, 2017 http://gizmodo.com/would-you-feel-safer-if-your-self-driving-car-could-exp-1795827465
- **Everyone keeps talking about A.I.—here's what it really is and why it's so hot now**, Jordan Novet, CNBC, June 17, 2017, http://www.cnbc.com/2017/06/17/what-is-artificial-intelligence.html
- **When Will AI Exceed Human Performance? Evidence from AI Experts**, Katja Grace, John Salvatier, Allan Dafoe, Baobao Zhang, and Owain, Evans, https://arxiv.org/pdf/1705.08807v1.pdf

- **A discussion about AI's conflicts and challenges**, Natasha Lomas, TechCrunch, June 17, 2017 https://techcrunch.com/2017/06/17/a-discussion-about-ais-conflicts-and-challenges/
- **The Real Threat of Artificial Intelligence**, Kai-Fu Lee, The New York Times, June 24, 2017, https://www.nytimes.com/2017/06/24/opinion/sunday/artificial-intelligence-economic-inequality.html
- **These Truckers Work Alongside the Coders Trying to Eliminate Their Jobs**, Max Chafkin and Josh Eidelson, Bloomberg Businessweek, June 22, 2017, https://www.bloomberg.com/news/features/2017-06-22/these-truckers-work-alongside-the-coders-trying-to-eliminate-their-jobs
- **Neuralink and the Brain's Magical Future**, Tim Urban, Wait But Why, April 20, 2017, http://waitbutwhy.com/2017/04/neuralink.html
- **Sprint: How to Solve Big Problems and Test New Ideas in Just Five Days**, Jake Knapp, Google Ventures, https://www.amazon.com/Sprint-Solve-Problems-Test-Ideas/dp/150112174X
- **An Open Letter to CEOs**, Alex Osterwalder & Yves Pigneur, http://blog.strategyzer.com/posts/2017/7/11/an-open-letter-to-ceos

AI&U Workshops

AI is a complex and ever evolving topic. Due to its technical nature, the plethora of available news, articles, blogs, interviews, and videos can make it at times difficult to follow and make sense of. When approaching AI for your business, we recommend taking a staged approach, with a diverse group of people from different departments.

In our Demystifying AI workshops, we usually set out with a half day workshop. We begin by reviewing the main concepts and evolution as well as cover examples and look how AI can help in business. We also recommend looking at many examples for inspiration and understanding. Furthermore, we also contribute an outlook of where the technology might go. This brings everyone up to speed and serves as a strong common ground for the next stage.

Following this, a thorough process of ideation is recommended to identify concrete opportunities for your company. For this we usually allocate a full day, using design thinking methods to come up with ideas, and rate them along the company's potential and goals. It makes sense at this stage to involve the relevant stakeholders, as a validation of ideas requires stakeholder buy-in. The later stages will require more resourcing and experiments, therefore you will want the responsible people on board early on.

Before you engage in concrete projects, we recommend that first validate the idea with experts and real customers. For this we often use the Google Venture SPRINT method, which allows you to validate big ideas in only 5 days (http://www.gv.com/sprint/). This involves a team of people from your organization to spend 5 days following a well-defined method, that has been proven in over 100 projects. This has the team defining the long-term vision, drawing a systems map, gaining input from external experts, sketching various solutions, selecting the most promising approach, building a prototype and testing it with real users. Google Venture SPRINTs for AI are engaging and a fun experience for the whole team. We have found them to be the best approach to carrying out a fast but thorough analysis and discovering the right solution for your company.

All three stages build upon each other and ensure that the members of your organization are well aligned in maximizing the benefits of AI. We are happy to help you in developing the right way for your organization in AI. Simply contact us.

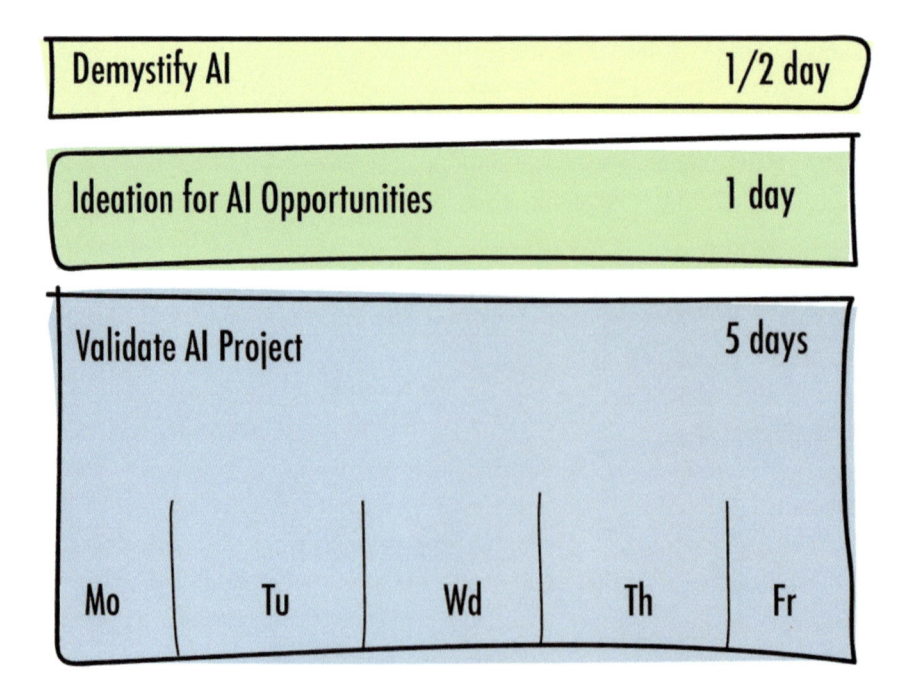

Demystify AI	1/2 day
Ideation for AI Opportunities	1 day
Validate AI Project (Mo, Tu, Wd, Th, Fr)	5 days

AI workshops by AI&U

About the Authors

Christian Ehl is an Internet activist and experienced entrepreneur with a passion for technology and how it transforms our lives and the way we do business. He is working to leverage Artificial Intelligence for a good future by working with various start-ups and corporations on AI projects. In addition to this, he is also involved in the Breakthrough Innovation work with the United Nations and the DO School. Christian is an active business angel and CEO of Hillert Interactive. He holds an electronics engineering degree from the Technical University of Munich and an MBA from Wake Forest University.

Sharad Gandhi is a technology philosopher and strategist for creating business value with digital technologies. By education, he is a physicist and electronics engineer and a marketing strategist by profession. He is a global citizen having lived and worked in Europe, USA and India for the best of companies —Intel, IBM, Siemens and Tata. In spite of being passionate about technology, he is aware and concerned about problems that technology creates. However, he believes that eventually technologies like the Internet, AI, robotics, biotech, genetics, new materials and space will help create innovations and solutions for many of our global problems in the environment, energy, inequality, poverty, health, and demography.

Printed in Germany
by Amazon Distribution
GmbH, Leipzig